SATAN:

His Personality, Power and Overthrow

SATAN:

His Personality, Power and Overthrow

By
EDWARD M. BOUNDS

BAKER BOOK HOUSE
Grand Rapids, Michigan

Reprinted 1972
by Baker Book House Company
ISBN: 0-8010-0586-8

Printed in the United States of America

Foreword

IN our mind's eye we can see Dr. Bounds, in the early years of the twentieth century, walking the streets of his own little village, with his manuscripts tied up with a twine string, and written upon the backs of old circulars, used envelopes, looking for some one who would undertake to prepare the manuscripts for publication and asking of his friends to pray that God would raise him up a man that would bring out his writings. Claudius Lysias Chilton, a scholarly friend of Dr. Bounds, said, "There is no man on earth to-day except the present editor who would have accepted this mass of matter and devoted the time to give it to the world—a world that will not begin to realize the magnitude and expanse of the work until editor, compiler and reviewers have been in eternity many ages."

We take this occasion to offer our heartfelt thanks to the friends who have helped to compile, revise, rewrite and edit the printed and unprinted works of Dr. Bounds. We thank Rev. Robert O. Smith, of Gainesville, Georgia, for introducing him to us in 1905, and pressing the matter upon us that we needed this apostolic man to teach us to pray and preach the Word. To one friend in particular—Rev. Clement C. Cary, of Atlanta, Georgia,—we owe the first expression of sincere gratitude for his part in this work. To him I am indebted for a vast amount of labour and study such as it can be the good fortune of few editors to receive from one so saintly and competent, occupied as he is by private and public duties. To Miss Ambrose, of Baltimore, Maryland, I am deeply indebted for splendid and correct stenographic work.

I here submit a few brief statements from Dr. Bounds' letters to me just before he died, which show his views of Satan ere he went far out of his reach.

"*Washington, Ga., Dec. 15, 1911:* I am trying to give myself more and more to prayer. Our only hope is in God. I do sympathize with you and pray for you and hold you in loving affection. Rejoice that you are well situated. God save you from your buffeting devil. The devil is a great help heavenward. The worse agents he has the better we will get on."

"*Washington, Ga., July 1, 1912:* Pray more and more; keep at the four A. M. hour. God will be for it; the devil against it. Press on, you can't pray too much, you may pray too little. The devil will compromise with you to pray as the common standard, on going to bed, and a little prayer in the morning. Hell will be full if we don't do better for God than that.

Pray, pray, pray, pray always, rejoice evermore, pray without ceasing, in everything give thanks."

It is barely possible that I have escaped making many errors involving so many examinations and rewriting so many pages in his published and unpublished works, but I still hope that many souls will be edified and made holier and more devout by the reading and that God will receive additional glory when Bounds' complete works have been given to a needy world.

HOMER W. HODGE.

Brooklyn, N. Y.

Contents

I

THE DEVIL: HIS BEGINNING

Satan hath here a mighty kingdom (Matt. 12:26), opposed to that of Christ in chapter 1:20, 21, consisting of men and angels, inhabiters of earth and air; wherein he had the start of Christ carrying the world before him, four thousand years previous to the incarnation. Zanchy, the most judicious of the protestant writers, and Suarez, the best of school-men, suppose with some probability, that the angels had notice of the setting up a kingdom for Christ (predestinated to come by the Second Person's assumption of human nature) and his therein being the head of all principality and power, from whom men and angels should have their grace; and that the sin of the fallen spirits was refusing subjection to this king; and that thus they "kept not their first estate but left their own habitation," voluntarily quitting that station God had set them in, and leaving their dwelling in heaven to go and set up an opposition kingdom here below.—*Thomas Goodwin.*

WE have no genesis of the devil in the Bible as a direct statement. The Bible is not his full history. It gives no intimation of his birth and no description of his creation. The Bible is only concerned with the devil as he has part in the great crises of man's history, and only gives us occasional glimpses of him in his work of ruin and death as explanatory, or as putting his acts in striking contrast and opposition to the works and aims of Christ. There

are not lacking in these intimations and infer-
ences, sidelights which indicate an original purity,
a high relation to God, and a heavenly character
and conduct. It is not a fanciful conjecture that
he was and is the head of the angels who kept not
their first estate. Peter in his first Epistle gives
the angel crises and fall as one of the signal events
which illustrate God's justice, its certainty and
fearfulness. He says, " God spared not the angels
that sinned, but cast them down to hell, and delivered them into chains of darkness to be reserved
unto judgment." Jude speaks after the same order
of God's inflexible wrath when he tells us that
" the angels which kept not their first estate, but
left their own habitation, he hath reserved in everlasting chains under darkness unto the judgment
of the great day."

The Revelation of John adds its testimony with
addition to this fact: "And there was war in
heaven; Michael and his angels fought against the
dragon; and the dragon fought and his angels, and
prevailed not; neither was there place found any
more in heaven. And the great dragon was cast
out, that old serpent, called the Devil, and Satan,
which deceiveth the whole world; he was cast out
into the earth, and his angels were cast out with
him."

To the Word of God we must go, assured that
we will find the traces of the devil's steps and the
unfolding of his conduct whose bad schemes have

eclipsed so much of earth's brightness and blasted so much of its promise and hope.

If we have the child-like spirit of docility and trust, if we will "lay aside all filthiness and superfluity of naughtiness, and receive with meekness the engrafted word," we will find satisfaction and illumination, not satisfaction as to curiosity, nor illumination in the niceties or subtilities of philosophy, but satisfaction and illumination in all things which pertain to the highest and weightiest truth for the thoughtful, trustful and prayerful mind.

In the Bible we have the facts and history of man's redemption. Incidentally or essentially, other worlds and other beings are brought prominently on the stage of redemption purposes and plans. These revealed facts whether incidental or essential, whether casual or regular, are to our faith what the facts of nature are to the student of nature. They must shape theories and settle opinions. They must not be set aside, for weighty and final they must be. Reason must not ignore nor reject them, but must lay them deep and solid as the foundation of all investigation, the basis of every hypothesis. These Bible facts demand our faith, though we may not be able to reach out beyond into the unknown regions where harmony reigns.

The Word of God brings clearly to light the unseen world, its persons, places, facts and history, not, we say, in minute detail, but full enough to provoke thought and reflection, and to create and inspire faith.

The Bible nowhere enters into an argument to prove the person and being of God. It assumes His being and reveals His person and character. Without preface or introduction, the Bible brings God before us in all His majesty and omnipotence. God is at the world's beginning, and He it was who created the beginning of all things. " In the beginning God created the heavens and the earth." How sublime and awe-inspiring our first glimpse of God! God is revealed not by argument but by work. We learn what He is from what He does.

In like manner is the revelation of the devil. He is before us in full person without introduction or ceremony as the evil one, a graduate in the work of guile and evil. The curtain is drawn and the chief actor is in full dress. A world is at stake, man is to be seduced, Eden is to be blasted. No light is shed upon his past history, no knowledge of the school where he learned his dire trade. He was before earthly life. Eden does not date his birth, and is not the first chapter of his history, nor is it the first trial of his hellish art. We have no access to the archives of the past. Eden bounds our horizon, and the devil is there. Henceforth his history is to run parallel with our race. Man is to be the object of his schemes, his ruin, and his ambition. Earth is to be the favourite scene of his exploits.   He is at the cradle of man, and has much to do in shaping his character and determining his destiny.

The Bible is a revelation, not a philosophy nor a poem, not a science.   It reveals things and persons as they are, living and acting outside the range of earthly vision or natural discovery.

Bible revelations are not against reason but above reason, for the uses of faith, man's highest faculty.   The powers of reason are not able to discover these Bible facts, and yet they are for reason's use, its light, strength and higher elevation, but more essentially to form, to nourish and to perfect faith.

The Bible reveals the devil as a person, not a mere figure, not an influence simply, not a personification only, but a real person.   In the eighth chapter of John, Christ is arraigning the cruelty and murderous malignity, the falsehood, deceit and hypocrisy of the Jews.   Jesus says, " Ye are of your father the devil, and the lusts of your father ye will do."   He was a murderer from the beginning and abode not in the truth, because there is no truth in him.

Many myths may have gathered around the person of the devil by the accretion of ages, much of poetry, sentiment and tradition, and even our fears may have caricatured his person, exaggerated his character, and coloured his conduct.   But there is truth in regard to him, naked and simple truth.

There is much truth that needs to be learned about the devil, and no age needs the plain, unvarnished truth about the devil more than this age. We need the light of that truth as a warning, as an incentive to vigilance, and an inspiration to effort. We need the knowledge of the enemy, his character, presence and power to arouse men to action, for this is vital to victory.

It is wholly at variance with any Christian idea of the perfection of truthfulness in Christ, who was truth itself, to suppose Him to have used such plain and solemn words repeatedly before His disciples and the Jews in encouragement and furtherance of a lying superstition.

A denial of the reality of demonical possessions on the part of any one who believes the Gospel narrative to be true and inspired, may justly be regarded as simply and plainly inconceivable.

When the devil fell, others fell with him. This is the lesson of God's Word.

Of the number of these fallen spirits we have no census. In Ephesians, quoting from the Revised Version, in the summary of these unseen foes we have " spiritual hosts," an uncounted, uncountable number.

How innumerable they are, we cannot tell. The demoniac of Gadara was named " legion because many devils were entered into him." A legion if exact was somewhat less than six thousand. Their number must be great, enabling them to spare so many to swarm into and possess one man, or even seven in one woman, as Mary Magdalene.

The statement in Revelation that the great red dragon with " his tail did draw the third part of the stars of heaven and did cast them to the earth," may be a reference to the fall of the angels and their number.

The Bible is clear in many references and some direct statements that the devil has a host of angelic followers who are ready, eager in their efforts to hurt man and defeat God's Kingdom on earth.

II

THE DEVIL: HIS PERSONALITY

Men don't believe in a devil now,
  As their fathers used to do;
They've forced the door of the broadest creed
  To let his majesty through;
There isn't a print of his cloven foot,
  Or a fiery dart from his bow,
To be found in earth or air to-day,
  For the world has voted so.

But who is mixing the fatal draft
  That palsies heart and brain,
And loads the earth of each passing year
  With ten hundred thousand slain?
Who blights the bloom of the land to-day
  With the fiery breath of hell,
If the devil isn't and never was?
  Won't somebody rise and tell?
                    —*Alfred J. Hough.*

THE devil is a person of marked emphatic character. Character gives dignity, place and value to the person, or character degrades the person. Character is that which is inner, cut in and graven. Character abides, forms action and shapes life. Character is a fountain. It is the head and stream of conduct; character often versus reputation. Character is what we are. Reputation is what folks think we are. The *real* and the *think so* are often two worlds. It would be well every way if reputation were based on character, if the real and the reputed were one. A bad reputation may be coupled with a good character. Then the times are sadly out of joint or the environments, and the folks are more sadly out of joint than the times. A good reputation may be but the veneering of a bad character. The devil has this characteristic with him. Reputation is based on character. They are one. His reputation is bad, because his character is worse.

The devil is *a created being*. He is therefore not self-existent nor eternal, but limited and finite. There was a time when he was not, when he began to be. His creation was after the order of the angels. The angels were not the offspring of the family relation. Cradlehood and all the tender ties, training, sweetness and growth are unknown to them. The pains and joys of child-birth are not theirs. Each angel is created, not born, created directly, personally, by God. The devil was created good, doubtless very good. His purity, as well as exaltation, were sources of congratulation, wonderment and praise in heaven.

The devil is *a positive character*. He wears disguises, but his ends are single and lie in only one direction, double-faced but never double-minded, never undecided, never vague nor feeble in his purposes or ends. No irresolution, nor hesitant depression nor aimless action spring from him. The devil has character if not horns, for character is often harder and sharper than horns. Character is felt. We feel the devil. He orders things, controls things. He is a great manager. He manages bad men, often good men and bad angels. Indirect, sinister, low and worldly, is the devil as a manager.

Is Christ a person? He puts the devil in opposition and contrast to Himself as a great mighty malignant person the sower of all evil—as Christ is the sower of all good. " The field is the world; the good seed are the children of the kingdom; but the tares are the children of the wicked one; the enemy that sowed them is the devil; the harvest is the end of the world; and the reapers are the angels."

Is Christ impersonal? Are the children of the kingdom impersonal? Are the children of the wicked one impersonal? Are not Christ and the children of the kingdom personal and persons? Are not the children of the wicked one and the devil personal and persons also?

In the Bible the personality of the devil is made emphatic. He is not only the source of evil to others, but the embodiment of evil in a person. The Revised Version makes this emphatic. The petition in the Lord's Prayer, " Deliver us from evil," becomes personal, " Deliver us from *the evil one*." So we find Christ praying not only that His disciples should be delivered from evil, all evil, impersonal and general, but " that thou shouldst keep them from the evil one." The statement by John that "the whole world lieth in wickedness," becomes personal, for in the Revised Version, all wickedness concentrates in a person. "The whole world lieth in the evil one." Here, too, the devil is called the "wicked one." Personality is attributed to him. Fatherhood is attributed to him, the father of all evil, the enemy of Jesus, malignant, active, crafty, cautious, cowardly.

The devil and his angels are of a higher order than the fallen sons of Adam, by rank, order, and intelligence. The devil is called in the Bible a prince, a world ruler, "prince of this world." He is designated as "the devil and his angels." He and they are held accountable, are condemned for their sins and for revolt in leaving their "first estate," the sphere for which they were created, and in which they were originally placed by God. This fact of their fall, and all the other statements, direct and incidental, emphasize them as persons, living, acting, free, accountable. That they had a chief prince in all their movements, prime in wisdom, prime in skill and in leadership, is clear from all Scriptural statements concerning the devil and his angels.

In 2 Corinthians 11: 13, Paul says: "For such are false apostles, deceitful workers, transforming themselves into the apostles of Christ. And no marvel; for Satan himself is transformed into an angel of light. Therefore it is no great thing if his ministers also be transformed as the ministers of righteousness, whose end shall be according to their works." "Satan himself" is an emphatic declaration of personality. He has ministers. An influence does not have ministers. Paul is writing of persons, wily, fraudulent and alluring, and he introduces the great person, the pattern and inspirer of all their fraud, hypocrisy and error, his apostles, false as he, the arch-impostor.

Jude has a statement which brings into view many persons: "Likewise also these filthy dreamers defile the flesh, despise dominion, and speak evil of dignities. Yet Michael, the archangel, when contending with the devil, he disputed about the body of Moses, durst not bring against him a railing accusation, but said, The Lord rebuke thee."

The "filthy dreamers" were persons. Moses was a great person. Michael an archangel was a person. The devil, what was he, if not a person? Living in the Mosaic dispensation, the devil was contending with the highest dignity under that dispensation of angels. Did the mighty archangel have to appeal for help against a mere influence, a shadowy, dreamy personification? This statement in Jude declares the devil to be a high dignity, whose person and presence are not to be treated with indignity or by frivolity or raillery.

The statement in Peter is after the same order and to the same end. The devil is a person of great dignity. "The Lord knoweth how to deliver the godly out of temptation, and to reserve the unjust unto the day of judgment to be punished. But chiefly them that walk after the flesh in the lust of uncleanness, and despise government. Presumptuous are they, self-willed, they are not afraid to speak evil of dignities. Whereas angels, which are greater in power and might, bring not railing accusation against them before the Lord. But these, as natural brute beasts made to be taken and destroyed, speak evil of the things that they understand not, and shall utterly perish in their own corruption."

Note how James puts the mightiest persons in contrast and opposition: " Submit yourselves therefore to God. Resist the devil and he will flee from you. Draw nigh to God and he will draw nigh to you." Why such a combination and contrast? Is God not a person? How can we then reduce him who is so in God's way to a mere influence? The passage teaches a personal devil as surely as a personal God.

Why are God and the devil in like manner conjoined in Peter's urgent exhortation? " Humble yourselves, therefore, under the mighty hand of God, that he may exalt you in due time; casting all your care upon him, for he careth for you. Be sober, be vigilant; because your adversary, the devil, as a roaring lion, walketh about, seeking whom he may devour." Why casting all care on Him? Why be sober and vigilant? " Your adversary" can be no less than a person against whom the Christian has to be armed with God. "Your adversary!" Hate and ruin are in his opposition. Can he be less than a person? The devil, "walking about like a roaring lion," strong, full of passions, and deadly hate! Can anything less than a person of infernal passion and infernal power answer this divine portraiture? To Peter the existence and person of this powerful adversary had a sad demonstration in his own experience. The words were still on his conscience and heart and memory. "Simon, Satan hath desired to have you that he may sift you as wheat."

In the directions in the Sermon on the Mount about swearing, affirmations and conversation, Jesus says, "Let your communication be Yea, yea; Nay, nay: for whatsoever is more than these is of the evil one."

Under the powerful operations of the cross and the Spirit, as well as the restraining influences of the Gospel, evil would soon be driven from the earth, branded and banned, were it not for the mighty personality and executive ability of the devil.

We find many references, hints and reminders of the power and person of the devil, coming out in the ministry of Christ. The name "devil" invests him with an infamous personality, and clothes him with all the deceit, craft and cruelty attaching to that name. By the name "Satan,"

Christ puts him as the adversary of God and man. By designating him as " the prince of this world," Christ recognizes his royal power and ruling authority for evil in this world. The devil's agency in the ills that affect the body is not merely hinted at, but comes out as being taken for granted.

How strenuous and ever continuing the conflict between the devil and Jesus, is learned by the Lord's prayer, that perfect and universal prayer which Jesus puts in the heart and lips of His people in all ages, for as we have seen, according to the Revised Version, that petition of conflict, peril, warning, and safety is, " Deliver us from the Evil One." Evil is comparatively harmless, feeble and inert without the presence of its mighty inspirer. Deliverance from the devil is deliverance from the many evils of which he is the source and inspiration.

In the sixth chapter of Ephesians, the Christian soldier-hood, its character, armour, conduct and courage are challenged, and he is urged, because of the devil's power, and because the Christian's warfare is mainly against him, to this effect: " Put on the whole armour of God, that ye may be able to stand against the wiles of the devil. For we wrestle not against flesh and blood, but against principalities, against powers, against the rulers of the darkness of this world, against spiritual wickedness in high places."

The Christian's comfort as administered by Paul in the sixteenth chapter of Romans is not only the impartation of, " The grace of the Lord Jesus Christ be with you," but also, "And the God of peace shall bruise Satan under your feet shortly."

Peter's vital exhortation has a double imperative in it, not only the " casting all our care on God," but a loud and urgent call to watch and pray. " Be sober, be vigilant; because your adversary the devil, as a roaring lion, walketh about, seeking whom he may devour." Peter recognized in the deadly crime of Ananias and Sapphira the hand of Satan, and remonstrates thus: "Ananias, why hath Satan filled thine heart to lie to the Holy Ghost, and to keep back part of the price of the land? "

The warning and exhortation which Christ sends to the Church at Smyrna to prepare and nerve to endurance involves the person and power of the devil. " Fear none of those things which thou shalt suffer; behold, the devil shall cast some of you into prison, that ye may be tried; and ye shall have tribulation ten days. Be thou faithful unto death, and I will give thee a crown of life." The explanation of the parable of the tares puts the malignity, person, and power of the devil in contrast with Christ. " The field is the world; the good seed are the children of the kingdom; but the tares are the children of the wicked one. The enemy that sowed them is the devil; the harvest is the end of the world; and the reapers are the angels."

The defense of Christ against the Pharisaic charge of violating the Sabbath puts the devil conspicuous in his work of evil: "And ought not this woman, being a daughter of Abraham, whom Satan hath bound, lo, these eighteen years, be loosed from this bond on the Sabbath day?"

The statement about Judas, "And supper being ended, the devil having now put into the heart of Judas Iscariot, Simon's son, to betray him;" is a statement not of an influence nor a personification, but of a person outside of Judas, making suggestions to him, and urging him on to his act of hypocrisy, and the suggestion is strictly in keeping with the character of the devil. "And after the sop Satan entered into him. Then said Jesus unto him, That thou doest, do quickly." How much an advance in fulness and power of action and influence is this act compared with his work in paradise! There he used a serpent as his instrument. Here a man, a chosen, trusted apostle. "A messenger of Satan," says Paul, " to buffet me." The exalted revelation and experience of the person and power of Christ are closely followed by the revelation and experience of the person and power of the devil.

The fearful doom of the wicked at the judgment is thus set forth by Christ: " Then shall he say also unto them on the left hand, Depart from me, ye cursed, into everlasting fire, prepared for the devil and his angels." The final doom of Satan is revealed in these words, "And the devil that deceived them was cast into the lake of fire and brimstone, where the beast and the false prophets are, and shall be tormented day and night for ever and ever."

These extracts are not only arguments to prove the existence or personality of the devil, but are logical conclusive references to a person whose being is taken for granted, universally accepted and thoroughly believed by them all.

A singular case would that mind be in its attitude to God's Word, who should profess to accept that Word and not believe in the existence of the devil. This would be a great breach both in the logic and faith of such a mind, as if the play of "Macbeth" were accepted in utter failure to recognize the person or existence of Lady Macbeth, whose character forms the entire plan and colour of the whole.

The encounters with those who were possessed of devils illustrates Christ's constant recognition of them as personal beings. He recognizes their distinct individuality. He talks to them and commands them as persons. They know Christ, confess His divinity, bow to His authority, obey, however unwillingly, His commands. He makes the clear distinction between the *human personality* possessed by the devil, and *the personality of the devil* who holds possession. The two are to his eye *two persons*.

That the exercising of these did give a severe blow to Satan's kingdom is declared by Christ's exclamation at the return and report of the seventy. " That even the devils are subject unto us through thy name." He exclaimed, " I beheld Satan as lightning fall from heaven," and then amid their ecstasy and His joy He renewed their commission. " Behold, I give unto you power to tread on serpents and scorpions, and over all the power of the enemy, and nothing shall by any means hurt you. Notwithstanding, in this rejoice not, that the spirits are subject unto you; but rather rejoice because your names are written in heaven." " Over all the power of the enemy." The devil is the enemy of Christ, of man. Power over all the devil's power.

To Christ the devil was one of the most real persons. He recognized his person, felt and acknowledged his power, abhorred his character, and warred against his person and kingdom.

III

THE PRINCE OF THIS WORLD

Now we come to the second guide in men's walk through life; and we see, first, The misery of all nature, in respect of subjection of Satan, who as a prince rules over and governs "the children of disobedience." Secondly, That Satan, as well as the world, is a cause of that sinfulness that is in the hearts and lives of men: they the exemplary and he the impelling cause, both as a prince and a spirit. Thirdly, A descriptive greatness of Satan's kingdom interwoven to shew man's misery the greater and the more; "the prince of the power of the air," the spirit that works in the children of disobedience." The scope of all these three particulars was to stir up the Ephesians' hearts to thanksgiving for the great deliverance, which in their conversion had brought them out of darkness into the light (out of the kingdom of darkness into the kingdom of His dear Son (Col. 1 : 13). Now the kingdom of power, glory experienced by the Church and Christ is the more endeared and enriched to us by our rescue from the empire of Satan and the world whose domain is the air and will end with the air, whereas ours are in heavenly places.—*Thomas Goodwin.*

TO the Holy Spirit, the substitute, representative and successor of Jesus Christ, was committed this work of breaking the deadly power of the world by breaking the power of its prince. There was the necessary and continuous reminder that the devil occupied the royal position of the world's prince, already adjudged and condemned, and upon whom the sentence and penalty were to be executed. "Nevertheless, I tell you the truth: It is expedient for you that I go away; for if I go not away, the Comforter will not come unto you; but if I depart, I will send him unto you. And when he is come, he will reprove the world of sin, and of righteousness, and of judgment; of sin because they believe not on me; of righteousness, because I go to my Father, and ye see me no more; of judgment, because the prince of this world is judged."

"The prince of *this world*" he is, though the awful doom awaiting unbelief, sin and unrighteousness are his.

In these declarations of Jesus Christ, we have the clear revelation of what the devil is in his relation to the world as a prince and ruler. We understand why the world is so alien to God, to God's Son, to His cause, and how attachment to the world is at once estrangement and bitter enmity to God, because in the world's beauty and charms there is the enmity of the devil to God. The world is the beauteous harlot with her snares of death and hell.

The devil is recognized by Jesus Christ to be the prince of this world, not lawfully, but in its rebellion against God, not to be submitted to, but to be renounced as a lawless one, dethroned as a usurper and conquered as a rebel. To secure these ends, to dethrone and conquer the devil, the mission of the Son of God is charged. We see how readily Jesus Christ acknowledges the position and power of the devil. It is of the devil He speaks, and conjoins him with the world. The stroke of the Son of God falls on both: " Now is the judgment of this world; now shall the prince of this world be cast out. And I, if I be lifted up, will draw all men to me." The world is condemned by the power of the cross. The sweet attractive potencies of the cross dissolve the fatal fascinations of the world. The power of that same cross casts out from his world ruling throne the prince of this world. Christ affirms the devil's high position, but signs and seals his destiny and doom. " God anointed Jesus of Nazareth with the Holy Ghost and with power; who went about doing good, and healing all that were oppressed of the devil, for God was with him."

Again does the Son of God recognize the position which the devil holds as crowned prince by the world's franchises. How his presence quiets the Son of God. Man's words are not to be victors in this conflict. God's words in the temptation broke the power of his assault and defeated his fell intents, but left him still a sovereign with his kingly crown. The Son of God is awed into silence at the devil's approach. The cross, its agony and shame, its deep humiliation, bitter agony and untold shame, its defeat and despair, all these it would take to lift the crown from Satan's brow and bring his throne down to dust and ashes. The adorable Son of God " saw the travail of His soul in that hour and was satisfied." He saw also what it would cost Him, and what it would cost every son of heaven, to discrown that prince, and He lapsed into a solemn silence, the prestige of His victory. "Hereafter I will not talk much with you, for the prince of this world cometh, and hath nothing in me."

IV

THE DEVIL A BUSY CHARACTER

We are apt to think that Satan is most powerful in crowded thoroughfares. It is a mistake. I believe the temptations of life are always most dangerous in the wilderness. I have been struck with that fact in Bible history. It is not in their most public moments that the great men of the past have fallen; it has been in their quiet hours. Moses never stumbled when he stood before Pharaoh, or while he was flying from Pharaoh; it was when he got into the *desert* that his patience began to fail. David never stumbled while he was fighting his way through imposing armies; it was when the fight was over, when he was resting quietly under his own vine and fig-tree that he put forth his hand to steal. The sorest temptations are not those spoken but those echoed. It is easier to lay aside your besetting sin amid a cloud of witnesses than in the solitude of your own room. The sin that besets you is never so besetting as when you are alone.—*George Matheson.*

IF there be any virtue in not being an infidel, the devil may claim this virtue. If it be any praise to be always busy, the devil may claim that praise, for he is always busy, and very busy. But his character does not spring from his faith. His faith makes him tremble, his character makes him a devil.

The devil is a very busy character. He does a big business, a very mean business, but he does it well, that is, as well as a mean business can be done. He has large experience, big brains, a black heart, great force, and tireless industry, and is of great influence and great character. All his immense resources and powers are laid out for evil. Only evil inspires his activities and energies. He never moves to relieve or bless, a stranger alike to benevolent doing and kindly feeling.

Satan's history antedates the history of man— the only beings, he and his angels, who know by sad experience, Heaven, Earth and Hell. These three words are familiar to him. He has walked the streets of Heaven side by side with its purest and best. He has felt the thrill of its purest joys. He knows the bitterest anguish of hell, and has felt its keenest flames.

He does a big business on earth. He is a prince and a leader. Men and devils are his agents, and the elements are often by him debauched from their benignant purposes, and are made to destroy. He is busy tempting men to evil. He has large experience in this business, and is an adept at it. By him sin loses its sinfulness, the world is clothed with double charms, self is given a double force, faith is turned into fanaticism and love into hate.

A spiritual character can work through agencies or directly on the spirit. He infuses thoughts, makes suggestions and does it so deftly that we do not know their paternity. He tempted Eve to take the forbidden fruit. He put it into David's mind to number Israel, thereby provoking the wrath of God. He influenced Ananias and Sapphira to lie to God. Peter's yielding to presumption was at his instance. Judas' betrayal was from the same baneful source. The temptation of Christ was a typical and master piece of his business in seeking to seduce our Lord from God, showing his power to array agencies and pleas, and to back these by all forms of sanctity and persuasiveness. He is blasphemous, arrogant and presumptuous. He slanders God to men and infuses into men hard thoughts of God. He intensifies their enmity and inflames their prejudice against Him. He leads them to deny His existence and to traduce His character, thereby destroying the foundations of faith and all true worship. He does all he can by insinuation and charges to blacken saintly character and lower God's estimate of the good. He is the vilest of calumniators, the most malignant and artful of slanderers. Goodness is the point of his constant attack. He says nothing good about the good, nothing bad about the bad. He is always at church before the preacher is in the pulpit or a member in the pew, to hinder the sower, to impoverish the soil, or to blast the seed, that is, when courage and faith are in the pulpit, and zeal and prayer in the pew. But if dead orthodoxy or live heterodoxy are in the pulpit, he then puts in his time elsewhere at some point of danger.

Christ expressly declared that some sickness, at least, was the direct infliction of Satan.

The devil goes about to do evil and oppress men, at every point the antagonist of Him who went about to do good and heal all that were oppressed of the devil. In some way he had power over death and worked a fearful work of bondage and fear and death. Through death, Christ works to destroy him that had the power of death, that is, the devil. He puts a thorn in Paul's flesh and makes a special effort and requisition for Peter. He directs the whirlwind, kindles the fire and orders the disease which overwhelm and devastate Job and his property. He arms the thieving Chaldeans and Sabines against him and gets into his wife, and directs the divers agencies of his empire to ruin this one saint. He will wreck an empire at any time to secure a soul. He sows the tares in the wheat, the bad among the good, bad thoughts among the good thoughts. All kinds of evil seed are sown by him in the harvest fields of earth. He is always trying to make the good bad and the bad worse. He fills the minds of a Judas and inflames and hurries him on to his infamous purpose. He fills Peter with an arrogant pride which tries to thwart the divine plans and to inject human views into the purpose of Christ instead of God's purpose.

The devil goes about as fierce, as resolute, and as strong as a lion, intent only to destroy, restrained by no sentiments which soften and move human or divine hearts. He has no pity and no sympathy. He is great, but only great in evil. A great intellect, he is driven and inspired by a malignant and cruel heart.

At the threshold of Christ's ministry there we meet with His temptations by the devil,—one of those conflicts on which one of the mightiest issues turn. The history of the case presents the devil as a spiritual person, the head and embodiment of all evil, making a fierce, most wily, and protracted assault on the Son of God. We are not informed as to what shape he assumed to veil the treachery and wickedness of his attack. The temptation is noted as one of the preliminary and pivot facts of Christ's ministry, and can no more be resolved into the visionary than can His baptism, the descent of the Spirit, His wilderness trip, or His fasting. It was no influence tempting Christ. The whole transaction forbids that. "He was led of the Spirit into the wilderness to be tempted of the devil." The devil came to Him and the devil left Him, and then "the angels came and ministered to him."

In this temptation the methods, hypocrisy and craft of the devil are seen. How materially and benevolently he comes to the weak, exhausted Son of God! How innocent is the suggestion that Jesus use His power to relieve His hunger! What could be more allowable than that? To use His spiritual power for temporal ends! How often is it done? What a world of evil to religion when it is used to subserve the natural. Man living for bread alone. The temporal the first. The secular and worldly prime. Religion not simply to serve money or business, but religion secondary or subservient to business. The heavenly used for the earthly, the spiritual for the natural, more intent on daily food than on daily grace, eyeing the seen more than the unseen. That is the devil's main business—to materialize, earthlyize religion, to get man to live for bread alone, to make earth bigger than heaven. Time is more engaging than eternity. What a fearful conflict is being carried on in that quiet wilderness between the fainting Son of God and Satan, between the earthly and the heavenly, between God's religion and the devil's religion!

The conflict surges around three points. The fleshly, the presumptuous and the worldly. But this little circle holds all the shapes and forms of temptation, all the crafty devices, all the hidden depths, all the glittering seductions which Satan has devised to swerve men from the lofty allegiance which faith demands. The devil's assault on Christ is in striking contrast with his temptation to beguile Eve, and in more striking contrast with his fearful ordeal through which he tried Job's integrity. No suspicion cast on God's goodness as with Eve, no terrific, curdling sorrow as in

Job's case.   All is friendly, sympathetic and inviting.

The second temptation includes in it, not merely the fanatical presumption of overheated zeal and brainless devotion, but all the methods of sensational and abnormal piety by all those short cut processes by which the severe and tedious principles of a genuine faith are set aside, and spurious, superficial and flesh-pleasing substitutes are brought in to make a more attractive and popular guise of faith.   It seeks to take man-devised methods, easy, fragrant of sentiment, rank and material, in the stead of God's lowly way of godly sorrow, strict self-denial, and prayerful surrender.

Then the last, the world, its kingdoms and its glory, these as the reward of his devotion to Satan, worship the devil, that is, the world's god.   How the devil massed all his forces!   Religion was invoked.   The world and the flesh all conspired, under Satan's power, to tempt the Son of God. With what reluctance the pure soul of the Son of God went unto this close conflict with Satan is seen in Mark's statement: " And immediately the Spirit driveth him into the wilderness." No wrestling can warp this statement into a mere influence.   It is history, fact—plain, simple, historical fact.   Reread the record as to the devil. How clearly, without a doubt or figure of speech, does it stamp the whole transaction with personality.   " Then was Jesus led up of the Spirit into the wilderness to be tempted of the devil. And he was there in the wilderness forty days tempted of Satan; and was with the wild beasts; and the angels ministered unto him. Then the devil leaveth him, and, behold, angels came and ministered unto him." These are not figures of speech, but the narrative of a transaction and of persons engaged in the transaction. The wilderness and the fasting are literal. The beings are all literal, the wild beasts, the angels, Jesus and the devil.

The conflict of Jesus with Satan is not incidental, nor accidental, nor casual, but essential and vital. Satan held man and man's world in thrall. They had fallen into his hands and were held by him in bondage and ruled by him with desperate power.

The record has been made, "And when the devil had ended all the temptation, he departed from him for a season."

The season has ended and he is back again as though he had brought seven other spirits more wicked than himself. Gethsemane is the sum of the devil's most maddened and desperate methods. The guises are off. He appears there as he is. It is a rare thing to get a clear, true light on the devil. He assumes so many rôles, acts so many parts, wears so many guises. Here we have him in life size and in perfect features. The air is heavier by his breath, the night is darker by his shadow, the ground is colder, and his chill is on it. Judas is falser still, and Peter more cowardly and dastardly, because Satan is there. On the threshold of Gethsemane he exclaims, " My soul is exceeding sorrowful unto death," and he began to be sore amazed and very heavy. Why? Because "this is your hour and the power of darkness." Why? Because "now is the judgment of this world: now shall the prince of this world be cast out." Silence is there, dread and horror, and a great darkness and a fearful conflict. Why? " For the prince of this world cometh and hath nothing in me."

How different the devil's method now with Christ than in the wilderness. Then there was mildness, an assumed sympathy, the spirit of an inquirer, one desirous to relieve. The most pleasant and attractive and satisfying ministries to flesh did Satan then offer, something of the gentleness of the lamb, the interest and sympathy of a friend. But now how changed! The lamb is transformed into the lion, a roaring lion, maddened and desperate. Jesus could not be seduced by the flesh, nor self, nor the world in the wilderness. He must be overwhelmed with dread and horror, and be driven. His steadfastness must be overcome by weakness and fear. So comes he to many a saint in the fierceness and power of the lion when the gentle inducements fail.

V

THE DEVIL AND THE CHURCH

The identification of Christ with men was as complete in extent as it was real in nature. The first chapter of the Epistle to the Hebrews sets forth seven proofs of Divine Sonship, and the second chapter enumerates the following seven points of His identification with man: He descended to man's level, took man's nature, endured man's temptation, died in man's place, conquered the devil, man's foe, achieved man's victory, and secured man's salvation.

—*Samuel Chadwick.*

THE devil is too wise, too large in mental grasp, too lordly in ambition, to confine his aims to the individual. He seeks to direct the policy and sway the scepter of nations. In his largest freedom, and in his delirium of passion and success, "he goes out to deceive the nations which are in the four quarters of the earth." He is an adept in deception, an expert in all guileful arts. An archangel in execution, he often succeeds in seducing the nations most loyal to Christ, leading them into plans and principles which pervert and render baneful all Christly principles. The Church itself, the bride of Christ, when seduced from her purity, degenerates into a worldly ecclesiasticism.

The " gates of hell shall not prevail " against

the Church. This promise of our Lord stands against every Satanic device and assault: But this immutable word as to the glorious outcome does not protect the Church from the devil's stratagems which may, and often do, pervert the aims of the Church and postpone the day of its final triumph.

The devil is a hydra-headed monster, but he is hydra-headed in plans and wisdom as well as in monstrosities. His master and supreme effort is to get control of the Church, not to destroy its organization, but to abate and pervert its Divine ends. This he does in the most insidious way, seemingly innocent, no startling change, nothing to shock nor to alarm. Sometimes the revolutionizing and destructive change is introduced under the disguise of a greater zeal for Christ's glory. Introduced by some one high in church honour, often it occurs that the advocate of these measures is totally ignorant of the fact that the tendency is subversive.

One of the schemes of Satan to debase and pervert is to establish a wrong estimate of church strength. If he can raise false measurements of church power; if he can press the material to the front; if he can tabulate these forces so as to make them imposing and aggregating in commands, influence, and demand, he has secured his end.

In the Mosaic economy, the subversion of the ends of the Church and the substitution of material forces was guarded against. Their kings were warned against the accumulation, parade, and reliance on material forces.

It was in the violation of this law that David sinned when he yielded to the temptation of Satan to number the people.

It was to this end some suggest that the devil contended with Michael, the archangel, about the body (or system) of Moses, referred to in Peter and Jude and narrated by Zechariah, third chapter. At which time there was given that redoubtable, rallying text which asserts the eternal separation of spiritual forces from and their antagonism to the material. *" Not by might nor by power, but by my Spirit,* saith the Lord."

To this, the third temptation of our Lord was directed. In measure, such temptation by which the devil tried Jesus was intended to subvert the ends of His kingdom by substituting material elements of strength for the spiritual.

This is one of the devil's most insidious and successful methods to deceive, divert and deprave. He marshals and parades the most engaging material results, lauds the power of civilizing forces and makes its glories and power pass in review till church leaders are dazzled, and ensnared, and the Church becomes thoroughly worldly while boasting of her spirituality. No deceiver is so artful in the diabolical trade of deception as Satan. As an angel of light he leads a soul to death. To mistake the elements of church strength, is to mistake the character of the Church, and also to change its character all its efforts and aims. The strength of the Church lies in its piety. All else is incidental, and is not of the strength of things. But in worldly, popular language of this day, a church is called strong when its membership is large, when it has social position, financial resources; when ability, learning, and eloquence fill the pulpit, and when the pews are filled by fashion, intelligence, money and influence. An estimate of this kind is worldly to the fullest extent.

The church that thus defines its strength is on the highway to apostasy. The strength of the Church does not consist of any or all of these things. The faith, holiness and zeal of the Church are the elements of its power. Church strength does not consist in its numbers and its money, but in the holiness of its members. Church strength is not found in these worldly attachments or endowments, but in the endowment of the Holy Ghost on its members. No more fatal or deadly symptom can be seen in a church than this transference of its strength from spiritual to material forces, from the Holy Ghost to the world. The power of God in the Church is the measure of its strength and is the estimate which God puts on it, and not the estimate the world puts on it. Here is the measure of its ability to meet the ends of its being.

On the contrary, show us a church, poor, illiterate, obscure and unknown, but composed of praying people. They may be men of neither power nor wealth nor influence. They may be families that do not know one week where they are to get their bread for the next. But with them is "the hiding of God's power," and their influence will be felt for eternity, and their light shines, and they are watched, and wherever they go, there is a fountain of light, and Christ in them is glorified and His kingdom advanced. They are His chosen vessels of salvation and His luminaries to reflect His light.

There are signs everywhere unmistakable and of dire import that Protestantism has been blinded and caught by Satan's dazzling glare.

We are being seriously affected by the material progress of the age. We have heard so much of it, and gazed on it so long, that spiritual estimates are tame to us. Spiritual views have no form nor comeliness to us. Everything must take on the rich colourings, luxuriant growth and magnificent appearance of the material, or else it is beggarly. This is the most perilous condition the Church has to meet, when the meek and lowly fruits of piety are to be discounted by the showy and worldly graces with which material success crowds the Church. We must not yield to the flood. We must not for a moment, not the hundredth part of an inch, give place to the world. Piety must be stressed in every way and at every point. The Church must be made to see and feel this delusion and snare, this transference of her strength from God to the world, this rejection of the Holy Ghost by the endowment of "might and power," and this yielding to Satan. The Church more and more is inclined not only to disregard, but to despise, the elements of spiritual strength and set them aside, for the more impressive worldly ones.

We have been and are schooling ourselves into regarding as elements of church prosperity only those items which make showings in a statistical column, and which impress an age given up to the materialization of secular facts and figures; and as the most vital spiritual conditions and gains cannot be reduced to figures, they are left out of the column and its aggregates, and after a while they will neither be noted nor estimated. If we do not call a halt and change our methods, the whole estimate of the strength of a church will be supremely worldly. However imposing our material results may be, however magnificent and prosperous the secular arm of the Church appears, we must go deeper than these for its strength. We must proclaim it, and iterate and reiterate it with increased emphasis, that the strength of the Church does not lie in these things.

These may be but the gilded delusions which we mistake for the true riches, and while we are vainly saying, "We are rich and increased in

goods," God has written of us that we are
"wretched, and miserable, and poor, and blind,
and naked." They will be, if we are not sleeplessly vigilant, but the costly spices and splendid
decoration which embalm and entomb our spirituality. True strength lies in the vital godliness
of the people. The aggregate of the personal holiness of the members of each church is the only
true measure of strength. Any other test offends
God, dishonours Christ, grieves the Holy Spirit,
and degrades religion.

A church can often make the fairest and best
showing of material strength when death in its
deadliest form is feeding on its vitals. There can
scarcely be a more damaging delusion than to judge
of the conditions of the Church by its material ex-
hibits or churchly activity. Spiritual barrenness
and rottenness in the Church are generally hidden
by a fair exterior and an obtrusive parade of leaves
and an exotic growth. A spiritual church converts souls from sin soundly, clearly and fully, and
puts them on the stretch for perfect holiness, and
those who are straining to get it, to keep it, and
to add to it.

This spirituality is not a by-play, not to be kept
in a corner of the Church, not its dress for holiday
or parade days, but it is its chief and only business.
If God's Church is not doing this work of convert-
ing sinners to holiness and perfecting saints in
holiness, wherever and whenever this work is not

blazing and conspicuous, wherever and whenever this work becomes secondary, or other interests are held to be its equivalent, then the Church has become worldly. Wherever and whenever the material interests are emphasized till they come into prominence, then the world comes to the throne and sways the scepter of Satan. There is no readier and surer way to make the Church worldly than to put its material prosperity to the front, and no surer, readier way to put Satan in charge. It is an easy matter for the assessments to become of first moment by emphasizing them till a sentiment is created that these are paramount. When collecting money, building churches, and statistical columns are to stand as evidences of real church prosperity, then the world has a strong lodgment, and Satan has gained his end.

Another scheme of Satan is to eliminate from the Church all the lowly self-denying ordinances which are offensive to unsanctified tastes and unregenerate hearts, and reduce the Church to a mere human institution, popular, natural, fleshly and pleasing.

Satan has no scheme more fearfully destructive and which can more thoroughly thwart God's high and holy purposes, than to transform God's Church and make it a human institution according to man's views. God's right arm is thereby paralyzed, the body of Christ has become the body of Satan, light turned into darkness and life into death.

Men who sit in apostolic seats often through a marvellous blindness, sometimes through a false attachment to what they deem truth, and for what they consider the honour of Christ, are found trying to eliminate from the system of Christ those painful, offensive, unpopular, and self-denying features to which it owes all its saving efficacy, and beauty and power, and which stamp it as divine.

We have a painful illustration most instructive and warning in Peter, recorded thus:

" From that time forth began Jesus to shew unto his disciples, how that he must go unto Jerusalem, and suffer many things of the elders and chief priests and scribes, and be killed, and be raised again the third day. Then Peter took him, and began to rebuke him, saying, Be it far from thee, Lord; this shall not be unto thee. But he turned, and said unto Peter, Get thee behind me, Satan: thou art an offense unto me; for thou savourest not the things that be of God, but those that be of men. Then said Jesus unto his disciples, If any man will come after me, let him deny himself, and take up his cross, and follow me. For whosoever will save his life shall lose it; and whosoever will lose his life for my sake shall find it. For what is a man profited, if he shall gain the whole world, and lose his own soul? or what shall a man give in exchange for his soul? For the Son of Man shall come in the glory of his Father with his angels;

and then he shall reward every man according to his works."

Here is a lesson most suggestive, a lesson for all times, a warning for each man, for all men, for church men, for saintly men and for apostolic men. An apostle has become the mouthpiece of Satan! Alarming, horrible, unnatural and revolting picture! An apostle, zealous for his Master's glory, advocating with fire and force a scheme which would forever destroy that glory! An apostle, the apostle Peter, Satan's vicegerent! The apostle who had but just made that inspired confession, " Thou art the Christ, the Son of the living God," which placed him in highest honour and commendation with Christ and the Church! Before the words of that divine and marvellous confession had died from his lips, this same apostle is the inflamed and self-willed advocate of views and plans which will render his confession a nullity, and raze the impregnable and eternal foundations of the Church.

Peter, a chief apostle, fathering and advocating schemes which would discrown Christ of His Messiahship, and bring heaven's favourite plan to a most disastrous and shameful end! How came this? What baneful impulse impels Peter? Satan has entered him and for the time being, has mastered his purposes, and so Christ reproves Peter, but in the reproof strikes a crushing blow at Satan. " Get thee behind me, Satan," a reminder and duplicate of the wilderness temptation. "Thou art an offense (a stumbling block) to me." The devil's trigger to catch Christ in the devil's trap— "Thou savourest not the things which be of God, but those that be of men." The devil is not in sight. Man appears and his views are pressed to the front. The things which men savour in church plan and church life are against God's plan. The high and holy principles of self-denial, of unworldliness of life, and of self-surrender to Christ, are all against men's view of religion, a losing thing with them. The devil does not seek to destroy the Church only indirectly. Men's views would eliminate all these unpopular principles of the cross, self-denial, life surrender and world surrender. But when this is done, the devil runs the Church. Then it becomes popular, cheery, flesh-pleasing, modern and progressive. But it is the devil's church, founded on principles pleasing in every way to flesh and blood. No Christ is in it, no crucifixion of self, no crucifixion of the world, no second coming of Christ, no eternal judgment, no everlasting hell, no eternal heaven. Nothing is in it that savours of God, but all that savours of men. Man makes the devil's church by turning Christ's Church over to men leaders. The world is sought and gained in the devil's church, but the man, the soul, heaven, are all lost, lost to all eternity.

The very heart of this disgraceful apostasy, this dethroning Christ and enthroning the devil, is to remove the Holy Spirit from His leadership in the Church and put in unspiritual men as leaders to plan for and direct the Church. The strong hands of men of great ability and men with the powers of leadership have often displaced God's leadership. The ambition for leadership and the enthronement of man-leadership, is the doom and seal of apostasy. There is no leadership in God's Church but the leadership of the Holy Spirit. The man who has the most of God's Spirit is God's chosen leader, ambitious and zealous for the Spirit's sovereignty, ambitious to be the least, the slave of all.

VI

THE DEVIL AND THE CHURCH
(*Continued*)

Sometime in the country I have stood and watched the village blacksmith at work, and for a long time could not make out the use of the little trip hammer. The big hammer I could understand, but why should the smith strike in turns the anvil and the iron puzzled me. One day I ventured to ask an explanation, and found that the little hammer regulates the stroke of the big one. The smith holds the glowing metal, turning it lest the stroke fall too often upon the same spot, directing the blows that they may descend at the right moment; turning, tempering, regulating till the metal is fashioned to the desired shape. So God holds the soul and regulates the stroke. Sometimes He makes the Devil His hammer-man. . . . Satan strikes to smash. God regulates the stroke, and turns His malice to our perfecting, and the Devil sweats at the task of fashioning saints into the likeness of Christ.—*Samuel Chadwick.*

THERE are two ways of directing the Church, God's way and the devil's way. God's way and man's way of running the Church are entirely at poles. Man's wise plans, happy expedients and easy solutions, are Satan's devices. The cross is retired, the world comes in, self-denial is eliminated, all seems bright, cheerful and prosperous, but Satan's hand is on the ark, men's schemes prevail, the Church fails under these taking, pet devices of men, and the bankruptcy is so complete that the court of heaven will not even appoint a receiver for the collapsed and beggarly corporation.

All God's plans have the mark of the cross on them, and all His plans have death to self in them. All God's plans have crucifixion to the world in them. But men's plans ignore the offense of the cross or despise it. Men's plans have no profound, stern or self-immolating denial in them. Their gain is of the world. How much of these destructive elements, esteemed by men, does the devil bring into the Church, until all the high, unworldly and holy aims, and heavenly objects of the Church are retired and forgotten?

One of these taking, man-savouring, Satanic devices is to pervert the aims of the Church after this manner of statement and effort, that the main object of the Church to-day is not so much to save individuals out of society, as to save society, not to save souls so much as to save the bodies of men, not to save men out of a community so much as to save men and manhood in the community. The world, not the individual, is the subject of redemption.

This popular, seductive and deadly fallacy entirely subverts the very foundation of Christ's Church. Its materializing trend is so strong that it will sweep away every vestige of the spiritual and eternal if we do not watch, work and speak with sleepless vigilance, tireless energy, and fearless boldness. The attitude and open declaration of much of the religious teaching we now hear is in the same strain and spirit which characterized Unitarian, Jewish, or rationalistic utterances half a century ago.

To save society is a kind of religious fad to which much enterprising, lauded church work is committed. Advanced thinkers and discoverers have elaborated the same idea. They seem not to realize their true condition, which is one of going back, and not going forward. This backward step entombs religion in the grave where Judaism has been buried all these centuries. It may well accord with the idle dreams of the worldly rabbis to think of regenerating the world and ignoring the individual.

The phrase " to save the world," has a pompous sounding; and right taking to flesh and blood is it for the Church to apply itself to bettering the temporal surroundings of the individual, and improve his sanitary conditions; to lessen the bad smells that greet his nose, to diminish the bacteria in his water, and to put granite in the pavement for him to walk on instead of wood or brick. All this sounds finely, and agrees well with a material age, and becomes practical in operation, and evident and imposing in results. But does this agree with the sublime dignity and essential aim of the Church? Do we need any Church to secure these ends? Councilmen of common talent, an efficient street commissioner, and the ordinary vigilance of the average policeman, will secure these results in their best way. It needs no Church, no Bible, no Christ, no personal holiness, to secure these ends, and this is the point to which all this vaunted advance tends. If the ends of the Church are directed to those results which can be as well or better secured by other agencies, the Church will soon be regarded as a nuisance, a thing to be abated by the most summary process.

The purposes of the Church of God rise in sublime grandeur above these childish dreams and effete philosophies. Its purpose is to regenerate and sanctify the individual, to make him holy and prepare him by a course of purifying and training for the high pursuits of an eternal life. The Church is like the seine cast into the sea. The purpose is not to change the sea so much as to catch the fishes out of the sea. Let the sea roll on in its essential nature, but the net catches its fishes. No bigger fools would ever be found than fishermen who were spending all their force trying by some chemical process to change the essential elements of the sea, vainly hoping thereby to improve the stock of the fish that they had not and never could catch. By this method, personal holiness, the great desideratum for church operation and ends, would be impossible, and heaven would be stricken from creed and life and hope.

To save the world and ignore the individual, is

not only utopian, but every way damaging. It is the process, fair and laudable in name, to save the world, but in results it is to lose the Church, or, which amounts to the same, making the Church worldly, and thereby unfitting her for her holy and sublime mission. Christ said that gaining the world and saving the man are antagonistic ends. Christ teaches Peter that his Satanic device would gain the world to and for the Church, but would lose the soul. Everything would seem thrifty to the cause when in reality all was death.

The Church is distinctly, preëminently and absolutely a spiritual institution, that is, an institution created, vitalized, possessed and directed by the Spirit of God. Her machinery, rites, forms, services and officers have no comeliness, no pertinency, no power, save as they are depositions and channels of the Holy Spirit. It is His indwelling and inspiration which make its divine being and secure its divine end. If the devil can by any methods shut the Holy Spirit out from the Church, he has effectually barred the Church from being God's Church on earth. He accomplishes this by retiring from the Church the agencies or agents which the Holy Spirit uses, and displaces them by the natural, which are rarely if ever the media of His energy. Christ announced the universal and invariable law when He said, " That which is born of the flesh, is flesh; that which is born of the Spirit, is spirit." The Church may have a holy preacher, a man of great prayerfulness, of great grace, filled with the Spirit. But if Satan can by any method retire him, and put a man of no prayerfulness, plausible, eloquent and popular, the Church may seem to have gained, but it has gained by the substitution of natural for spiritual forces, a gain which has all unconsciously revolutionized the Church. Officer a church with holy men, not highly cultured, but well-versed in the deep things of God, and strong in devotion to Christ and His cause, not wealthy, nor of high social position. Now change these officers and put in men who are every way decent in morality, but not given or noted for prayer and piety, men of high social position and fine financiers, and the Church scarcely marks the change save marked improvement in finances. But an invisible and mighty change has taken place in the Church, which is radical. It has changed from a spiritual Church to a worldly one. The change from noonday to midnight is not more extreme than that.

At this point Satan is doing his deadliest and most damning work, the more deadly and damning because unnoticed, unseen, producing no shock and exciting no alarm.

It is not by positive, conspicuous evil that Satan perverts the Church, but by quiet displacement and by unnoticed substitution. The higher is being retired, the spiritual gives place to the social, and the divine is eliminated, because it is made secondary.

The perversion and subversion of the Church is secured by Satan when the spiritual forces are retired or made subordinate to the natural, and social entertainment, and not edification becomes the end. This process involves not only the aims and ends of entertainment, but it is intended to soften and modify the distinctly spiritual aim, and to widen from what is deemed the rigid exclusiveness of spiritual narrowness. But in the end it eliminates all that is distinctly spiritual, and that which is in any sense deeply religious will not survive the death of the spiritual. Edification as the end of God's Church is wholly lost sight of, and entertainment, that which is pleasing and pleasant, comes to the front. The social forces not only retire the spiritual forces, but effectually destroy them.

A modern church with its kitchen and parlour, with its club and lyceum, and with its ministries to the flesh and to the world, is both suggestive and alarming. How suggestive in the contrast it presents between the agencies which the primitive Church originated and fostered, as the conserver of its principles and the expression of its life, and those which the modern and progressive Church presents as its allies or substitutes. The original institutions were wholly spiritual, calculated to strengthen and cultivate all the elements which combine to make a deep and clear experience of God. They were training schools for the spiritual life, subservient to its culture as the chief end. They never lingered in the regions of the moral, the æsthetic and the mental. They fostered no taste nor inclination which was not spiritual, and did not minister to the soul's advance in divine things.

They took it for granted that all who came to them, really desired to flee from the wrath to come, and were sincerely groaning after full redemption, and that their obligation to furnish to these the best aids were of the most sacred and exacting kind. It never occurred to them that the lyceum or sociable were channels through which God's grace would flow and could be laid under tribute for spiritual uses. These social and fleshly forces are regarded in many quarters as the perfection of spiritual things. These agencies are arrayed as the mature fruit of spiritual piety, flavoured and perfected by its culture and progress, and ordained henceforth as the handmaids of the prayer and testimony meeting. We object most seriously to the union. What have they in common? "How indeed can two walk together unless they be agreed?"

What elements of piety are conserved by the lyceum or sociable? What phases of spiritual life do they promote? By what feature of the lyceum is faith invigorated? Where do you find in it any elements which are distinctly pious, or are aids to piety? How does the sociable produce a more prayerful, a holier life? What secret springs has it to bring the soul nearer to God? Wherein does it form or strengthen the ties of a Christly fellowship? Is it not frivolous and worldly? Is it not sensuous and fleshly? Does it not cater to and suit the tastes of the carnal, the light and worldly? What unity of purpose and spirit is there between the lyceum and witnessing for Christ? The one is intensely spiritual. The other has in it no jot or tittle of spiritual uses.

We might as well add to the list of heavenly helpers, the skating rink, calisthenics and the gymnasium. If the young people desire to join a lyceum, enjoy a sociable or establish a bank, let them do so, but do not deceive them and degrade piety by calling these things holy institutions and feeders of spiritual life.

Disguise it as we may; reason about it as we will; apologize for it as we do; vainly philosophize of growth and change and culture, the truth is, we have lost that intense type of personal experience, that deep conviction of eternal things which are such evident features of all great spiritual movements. Many preachers and people have fallen so low in their experience that they do not relish these distinct and strongly spiritual agencies; and are devising schemes and institutions to gratify their non-spiritual tastes with schemes which are midway between Christ and the world; which, while not essentially wrong, do not possess one grain of spiritual power, and can never be the channels of heavenly communications.

It is said we cannot get the people to attend the distinctly spiritual means of grace. What is the trouble? Are the institutions worn out and no longer of value to the humble, pious soul? Who will dare affirm this? The tastes of the people are low and perverted. Shall we then change the agencies to suit the unsanctified appetites? No; let us tone up the appetite for spiritual things, and correct and elevate the tastes of our people. Let the revolution begin with the preacher. Let him wrestle with God until his ordination vow becomes vitalized, so that all can feel the pressure of his aim, the ardour of his zeal, his singleness of purpose, and the holiness and elevation of his life, and until the people catch the fire and purpose of his heart, and all press on to the regions of perfect love, panting for all the fulness of God. Under this united, mighty, divine impulse the social and the lyceum will be forgotten and become stale, and all saintly assemblies will be attractive and delightsome.

The Church cannot confederate with non-spiritual agencies. By this she breaks the tension of her faith and discards the Holy Ghost. She cannot be the purveyor to unsanctified desires. Neither is it her province to fall down to the beggarly task of entertaining the people. This is her saddest mistake, when her solemn assemblies are surrendered to the concert and lecture, her praise turned into worldly music, her classrooms into parlours, her sociables more popular than her prayer-meetings, the house of God made a house of feasting, and social cheer is sought after rather than a house of prayer. The unity of the Spirit and the holy brotherhood are displaced and destroyed to make room for social affinities and worldly attractions. Her high and royal duty, that by which she maintains her spotless fidelity to her Lord, is to stress holiness and afford all means for its advancement and perfection. This done, spiritual character and affinities will order all the rest.

VII

THE DEVIL AND THE WORLD

By the "power of the air" is meant not simply in the abstract, Satan's government over the air whereof he is prince, but his devils, his angels that live and fly up and down in the air as the most convenient place for their residence; these have that power whereof he is prince; and as the "power of the air" refers to those airy spirits that are principalities and powers and rulers with him in this world, and who work under him in the men of this world; and they are a united kingdom, a body politic under this one prince, Satan: and they are called POWER, as we call an army a power, a force, as Pharaoh's host in Exodus 14:28; 15:4. The whole creation above the earth may be divided into three parts, whereof each part has its *powers* that are its inhabitants; there are the highest heavens, where is God and His host of angels; there are the starry heavens, with the sun for the prince of its hosts, and there is the air of this sublunary world, with Satan's trained crew there, called the "power of the air" or hosts of devils in the air under their prince.—*Thomas Goodwin.*

THERE is no more fundamental statement than that the world is to be renounced by every true disciple of Christ, and that to love the world and the things of the world puts us in open and standing enmity to God. By virtue of the relationship of love or friendship to the world, we are the enemies of God. There needs no other sin, no other crime by virtue of our attachment to the world. By that alone, we are the enemies of God.

Christ Jesus lays it down as an obvious truth that between the world and His disciples there would be hatred. The two discipleships to Himself and to the world were inimical and impossible. The call, the touch and choice of Christ when accepted and obeyed, becomes at once the secret and the source of the world's hatred.

Jesus declares the native and inevitable enmity of the world to His followers: " The world hath hated them because they are not of the world even as I am not of the world." Again, in the sacerdotal prayer, He declares this distinct and eternal separation and conflict: " They are not of the world, even as I am not of the world." By virtue of their relation to Christ they are separated from and are in conflict with the world.

The two persons, Jesus and Adam, their natures, affinities and opposition, are declared in the clearest language: " The first man is of the earth, earthy; the second man is the Lord from heaven. As is the earthy, such are they also that are earthy; and as is the heavenly, such are they also that are heavenly. And as we have borne the image of the earthly, we shall also bear the image of the heavenly." How strong is the opposition to the world declared and demanded. The love of the world is hostile to and destructive of the love of God. The two cannot co-exist.

" Ye adulteresses, know ye not that the friendship of the world is enmity with God? Whosoever therefore would be the friend of the world maketh himself an enemy of God" (R. V. James 4:4).

Nothing is more explicit than this, nothing is more commanding, authoritative and more exacting. " Love not the world." Nothing is more offensive to God, nothing is more criminal, more abominable, violative of the most sacred relationship of the soul with God. " Adulteresses "— purity gone and shame and illicit intercourse exist. Friendship for the world is Heaven's greatest crime and God's greatest enemy.

The world is one of the enemies which must be fought and conquered on the way to heaven. " For this is the love of God, that we keep his commandments; and his commandments are not grievous. For whatsoever is born of God overcometh the world, and this is the victory that overcometh the world, even our faith. Who is he that overcometh the world, but he that believeth that Jesus is the Son of God? "

The Gospel is represented as a training school in which to deny worldly desires is one part of its curriculum. " For the grace of God that bringeth salvation hath appeared to all men, teaching us, that denying ungodliness and worldly lusts, we should live soberly, righteously and godly, in this present world; looking for that blessed hope, and the glorious appearing of the great God and our

Saviour Jesus Christ; who gave himself for us, that he might redeem us from all iniquity, and purify unto himself a peculiar people, zealous of good works." There is something somewhere in the world which makes it a deadly foe to the salvation of Christ and which poisons us against heaven.

What is "this world," which so effectually alienates us from heaven and puts us by virtue of our relation to it and in flagrant enmity to God, and friendship to which violates our wedding vow to God, whose love is enmity to God, whose friendship is criminal to the most abominable and utmost degree? What is it? "The world, the lust of the flesh, the lust of the eye, the pride of life." What are they? The world includes the whole mass of men alienated from God, and therefore hostile to the cause of Christ. It involves worldly affairs, the aggregate of things earthly, the whole circle of earthly goods, endowments, riches, advantages, pleasures, and pursuits, which although hollow, frail and fleeting, stir desire, seduce from God, and are obstacles to the cause of Christ. The divorced or torn relation between heaven and earth, between God and His creatures, finds its expression in the term, "the world."

Our English word, "desire," expresses the meaning of the word *lust*, including the whole world of active lusts and desires, to which the seat of desire and the natural appetites impels.

Alford's Commentary says: "The world was

constituted at first in Adam, well pleasing to God and obedient to Him. It was man's world, and in man it was summed up, and in man it fell into the darkness of selfish pursuits, and by which man has become materialized in spirit and dragged down so as to be worldly and sensual. The world is man's world in his fall from God. The "lust of the flesh," human nature averse to God; "lust of the eyes," that sense which takes note of outward things and is inflamed by them. The "pride of life," the manner of life of worldly men among one another whereby pride is to display and pomp is cherished.

Bengel says: "The lust of the flesh" means those things on which the sense of enjoyment, taste and touch, feed. "Lust of the eyes" means those things by which the senses of investigation, the eye and sight, hearing and smelling, are occupied. "Pride of life" means when any one assumes too much to himself in words or actions. Even those who do not love arrogance of life may possibly pursue the "lust of the eyes," and they who have overpowered this yet frequently retain the lust of the flesh, for this prevails in the greatest degree and to the widest extent among the poor, the middle classes and the powerful, even among those who appear to exercise self-denial."

John Wesley says: "The desire of the flesh means the pleasures of the outward senses, whether of taste, smell or touch. The 'desire of the eye,' the pleasures of the imagination (to which the eye chiefly is subservient), of that internal sense whereby we relish what is grand, new or beautiful. The 'pride of life' means all that pomp in clothing, houses, furniture, equipage and manner of living which generally procure honour from the bulk of mankind, and so gratify pride and vanity. It therefore directly includes the desire of praise and remotely covetousness. All these desires are not from God, but from the prince of this world."

This world arrays itself and all its forces against heaven. Worldliness is the epidemic foe to heaven. To live for this world is to lose heaven by counter attraction. The Son of God declares of His disciples, and reiterates the declaration to His Father as one of prime importance: "Thou gavest them me out of the world. They are not of the world, even as I am not of the world." It remains true to this hour that all the true disciples of Jesus are not of the world, but are chosen out of the world, have left the world, have renounced the world, and are crucified to the world.

Fundamental and eternal are these truths, of which heaven has an illustration in every follower of Jesus.

What gives the world its fatal charms? What makes its witchery so deadly? Sometimes its beauty is all withered, its brightness all night, its hope all despair, its joy the bitterest anguish, and all its prospects decay and desert, but still it holds and binds. We are loath to leave it. Whence is its deadly sorcery and its fatal snares? Whence is its malignant hate? Whence is its hostility to God and its alienation from heaven? This world is the devil's world. In that fatal hour when man fell from his allegiance and devotion to God, he carried the world with him in his rebellion against God. Man was the world's lord, and it fell with its lord. This is the solution of its full influence, its malignant rivalry, and its intense opposition to heaven. The devil has his kingdom here. It is his princedom. He clothes it with all beauty and seductive power as the rival of heaven. Heaven's trinity of foes are the world, the flesh, and the devil. The world is first, the most powerful and engaging. They all center in and are strong for evil because the devil inspires and inflames them. The flesh wars with the spirit simply because the devil inflames its desires. The world gets its deadly and fascinating snares from the devil. The world is not simply the ally, but is the instrument and the agent of Satan. It represents him with the most servile and complete loyalty.

The text from John already quoted, "Love not the world, neither the things that are in the world," needs, for its full understanding, to have the preface which reads: "I write unto you, young men, because ye have overcome the wicked one. I write unto you, little children, because ye have known the Father. I have written unto you, fathers, because ye have known him that is from the beginning. I have written unto you, young men, because ye are strong, and the Word of God abideth in you, and ye have overcome the wicked one."

To "overcome the wicked one," the world, its love and its things must be abjured. There stands at the threshold of many a church door these words, which in spirit belong to the sacred honour of every soul's true espousal to Christ: "Dost thou renounce the devil and all his works, the vain pomp and glory of the world, with all covetous desires of the same, and the carnal desires of the flesh, so that thou wilt not follow or be led by them?" "I renounce them all," was the answer solemnly said in the serious hour, and the preacher and the people and our own hearts, if true, said, "Amen." And Amen let it be now and forever.

This world must be renounced and this is to renounce Satan. This is the deadliest blow at his rule. The friendship of the world is violative of our marriage vows to heaven.

We will not understand James in his severe denunciations of the world, where he makes its friendship so criminal and declares that to be the friend of the world is of itself to be the enemy of God, except we note how he is declaring that the world's friendship is the devil's religion, earthly, sensual, devilish; and that we can get back to God only by renouncing the friendship of the world and by cleansing our hearts and hands of its soiling touch. We draw nigh to God by resisting the devil. We resist the devil by renouncing the world.

The Apostle James sums up the distinct characteristics of the devil's world-counterfeit religion. Passion, appetite and pleasure reign and make war. How much of this passion, pleasure and world-religion has there been in church annals? Too often its history is a history of passion, strife, ambition and blood. Its ecumenical councils are the battlefield of passion in its unbridled, most malignant form. "Earthly, sensual, devilish," is the Divine stigma put on it, and obloquy is put on much of that which marks and mars ecclesiastical history. What volumes of this worldly religion, unwritten volumes, a world full of volumes, belong to the lives of many old reputed saints and to many modern church members and church goers. They are friends of the world, its advocates and lovers. They do not pray and only say prayers in order not to miss praying. There is no drawing nigh to God and no fighting against the devil and driving him from the field of action. Their religion and its performances and worship descendeth not from above, but is "earthly, natural, devilish." "Submit to God" and "resist the devil," is the keynote of an unworldly religion. A personal God and a personal devil are among the primary articles of creed and experience in true religion. Surrender to God, draw nigh to Him, live close to Him, fight against the devil, and get rid of him by denouncing and abjuring the world.

VIII

THE DEVIL AND THE WORLD (*Continued*)

Hesiod, speaking of the devils, saith, "Being clothed with air, they run up and down." By AIR is here meant this elementary sublunary world, and especially the airy part of it, that interstice between heaven and earth. All the Devil's workmanship in apparitions and visions is air condensed: he took Christ up into an exceeding high mountain, to make an outward representation wherein his power lay. Beelzebub signifying "god of flies" might allude to the air being as full of devils as it is of flies; certainly they are called "fowls of the air" (Luke 8: 5–12). Frantzius reports that a holy man in Germany on the night of the great massacre in France saw many spirits in the air, and was thereby assured of some great thing done in the world on that night. When angels come to minister they are compared to the meteors of the air, as in Psalm 104:4, "He makes his angels spirits, and his ministers a flame of fire." Now the air is only a place passage to angels, but it is the region wherein devils fly up and down, except where they possess men's bodies.—*Thomas Goodwin.*

THE divine warning against the course of the world, against the fashion of the world and against the spirit of the world, finds its solution in the fact that the devil is directing the world's course, the devil is creating the world's spirit, and the devil is cutting the pattern of the world's fashion. The touch of the world pollutes because Satan's fingers are in its touch. Its desires are deadly and heaven-quenching because Satan kindles its desires. The world and its things are contraband in the Christian warfare because Satan is the ruler of the world and the administrator of its affairs.

In Ephesians, Satan and his legions are called the "world-rulers." We quote from the Revised Version: "Put on the whole armour of God, that ye may be able to stand against the wiles of the devil. For our wrestling is not against flesh and blood, but against the principalities, against the powers, against the world-rulers of this darkness, against the spiritual hosts of wickedness in heavenly places." The "world-rulers" are principalities and powers under the direction of the devil. How they rule this world by ruling the things which rule this world! How Satan seizes and directs all the mighty forces of this world! War he seizes, and instead of it being the patriot's struggle for freedom and for the defense of home and native land, it becomes the pliant tool of despotism, crushes liberty and right, enslaves freedom, and carries on a campaign of lust, rapine, cruelty, desolation and death.

Money is another of the world's ruling forces which might be used to Edenize earth and to lay up a good foundation against the time to come. It ought to be used to ease the burdens of the poor, to banish beggary, and to brighten the homes of widowhood and orphanage. A mighty world-ruling power is money. The devil rules it and instead of flowing at the command of pitying love, it is diverted by Satan to all selfish and unholy purposes. Inflaming into covetousness and hardening into callousness, men become noted, illustrious and esteemed, as they are money-getters and money-keepers.

Education, a mighty world-ruling force, Satan chains this to his car, and it becomes the source of pride and ungodly power, and its mighty engineering is turned into "higher criticism," and under the guise of Christian learning, it becomes the most powerful ally to Satan, unsettling faith in God's Word in multitudes of hearts, and opening a wide door of skepticism in the temple of God.

In Ephesians the devil is called the "prince of the power of the air." The very atmosphere of this world ministers to his cause and is under his baneful rule. How much of storm and cyclones, terror and ruin is he responsible for we may not know. "And you hath he quickened who were dead in trespasses and sins; wherein in time past ye walked according to the course of this world, according to the prince of the power of the air, the spirit that now worketh in the children of disobedience. Among whom also we all had our conversation in times past in the lusts of our flesh, fulfilling the desires of the flesh and of the mind; and were by nature the children of wrath, even as others." "Among whom we all had our conversation," says Paul of himself and the saints. They formerly lived in Satan's kingdom, and he ruled them by the lusts of the flesh, " fulfilled the desires of the flesh and the mind." We see in this how Satan rules through the world. He is the god of this world, and by the world he excites its desires, both low and high, low in the desires of the flesh, and high in the desires of the mind. Whether the world fills the passions or appetites, or draws out and chains the mind in its high worldly pursuits and refined tastes, it is all of Satan, because of the world. The "lust of the flesh, the lust of the eyes and pride of life," these are of the world, and Satan is the exciter of them, " and lust when it is finished bringeth forth death."

" We know that whosoever is begotten of God sinneth not, but he that was begotten of God keepeth him and the evil one toucheth him not. We know that we are of God and the whole world lieth in the evil one " (Revised Version). The world " lieth," means that it is in the power of the devil, is held in subjection by him, and is fixed and established. The devil is pictured not only as trying to kindle into a flame the desires which may remain in a good man's heart after conversion, but also as folding in his arms the whole world and making it subject to his power and submissive to his absolute control.

When the world comes in at many a door, it comes in in many a form, but at whatever door and in whatever form it comes, it is always as the devil's servant. It comes in to do his work as his most obsequious and faithful slave. When the world comes in, dressed in its most seductive and beautiful garb, the devil has fashioned its clothing and ordered its coming. The world is the devil's heaven. Its rest, crown and good are here. When the world comes in, God's heaven goes out. It fades from the eye and heart. The struggle for it ends, and God's heaven, with its fadeless and eternal glories, is lost.

In these declarations of the Bible about the world and the devil, we see why the world opposes heaven. We learn the enmity of the two. Heaven is Christ's place, the place where He is, and to which He would win men. The world is Satan's place. His power is here. To fix our hearts on the world, is to be loyal to him. To fix our hearts on heaven, is to be loyal to Christ.

Here we have the solution of the cruel hatred of the world to Jesus and why it has persecuted so bitterly and to death His followers. We see why it is that the Spirit lusteth against the flesh and the flesh against the Spirit, and likewise we see why these are not only contrary to one another, but at war with one another. The devil is in the flesh and rules it. Christ is in the Spirit. This world leads from Christ. It is the invincible foe of Christ.

This great truth is illustrated and enforced by the fact that Christ's work is to get possession of the world and make its attractive power further

His purposes. But He establishes a kingdom of heaven which is not of this world. A new power has come in, a new kingdom established and a new world made. It will take the fires of the judgment and the new creative power to make a new heaven and a new earth before the stains and ruin of the devil's debasing and death-dealing hands can be removed, and this alien and hell-debauched, yet beautiful, world fitted for God's holy purposes.

The Christian, by the urgent demand made upon him to forswear allegiance to the world, is, by his very relation to Jesus Christ, lifted out of the world's deadly embraces, and its polluting witcheries are broken. In this subserviency of the world to the devil, we have the solution of the world's intense hatred to Jesus Christ, and we see why it has armed itself with all its forces under the power of the devil to destroy the cause of Christ. The world's opposition and enmity have been always against true religion, but often its smiles are more fatal than its hate.

IX

THE POWER OF THE DEVIL

This kingdom and these angels of Satan have great power; they are therefore called the "power of the air." We wrestle not against flesh and blood (the power of kings and armies and men are nothing) but against principalities, and powers, against spiritual wickedness; against devils that infinitely exceed all the sons of men: and the word is not only DUNAMIS, physical power of understanding, insinuation, but EXOUSIA, authority. If God had not given this great enemy so long, and so great, and so extensive a power to set up himself, His Son's kingdom had not been so glorious in the overthrow of it. O the mercy of God in translating us from the one to the other; we are pulled from the power of darkness by redemption (Col. 1 : 13), and by Christ Himself being subject to the power of Satan as in Luke 22 : 53 where the wicked have their hour but the saints shall have their day of it.—*Thomas Goodwin.*

IN all we have seen, instead of minifying the power of the devil, Jesus exalts him to the pinnacle of power as a prince, with this world as his princedom.

In the prominent features of Christ's life the devil appears as the one being and the one evil agent which Christ has in mind, to whose rule He is opposed. We have seen how soon the devil followed in the wake of our Lord's baptism at the Jordan, after the anointing of the Holy Ghost, and His public entrance on His ministry. When He first commissioned His disciples, among other great miracles they were to "cast out devils." When the seventy returned to report their work to Christ, they said, with evident surprise and gratulation, "Even the devils are subject to us through thy name." He replied: "I beheld Satan as lightning fall from heaven." When He is opening their hearts to receive the great comfort of that great promise of the Holy Spirit, He declares that one of the trinity of great ends to be executed by the Holy Spirit was "to convict the world of judgment, because the prince of this world is judged."

In one of His troubled and impassioned outbreaks, as the shadows and pain of His great agony are coming on Him, He cries, "Now is my soul troubled." The darkness is relieved by a gleam of light in which He sees the ruins of Satan's kingdom and the devil spoiled, dethroned, cast out by the almightiness of His cross, "Now is the judgment of this world; now shall the prince of this world be cast out. And I, if I be lifted up from the earth, will draw all men unto me."

But as the darkness grows deeper, and the anguish more bitter, He sees the approaching form of him whose hour and power of darkness it is. Hushed into silence in the presence of this relentless and cruel foe, the Son of God says to His sorrowing and awe-struck disciples: "Hereafter I will not talk much with you; for the prince of this world cometh, and hath nothing in me."

The devil's sad and mighty influence is farther set forth on the circle of chosen disciples. Peter staggers under the blow of the devil; his narrow, shameful escape of Peter is thus referred to by Christ: "Simon, Simon, behold, Satan hath desired to have you, that he might sift you as wheat: but I have prayed for thee, that thy faith fail not: and, when thou art converted, strengthen thy brethren."

Jesus Christ acknowledges the great power and authority which the devil has in the present deranged and usurped order of things. He declares, "Now is the judgment of this world, now shall the prince of this world be judged."

How defiant Satan is, and how he opposes Christ stubbornly with reckless and too often successful courage is plainly revealed. Into the chosen circle of the twelve he entered, into the one who had been trusted as their treasurer, the receiver, the depositor and the disburser of their money and their charity.

How close he comes, and how large his successes! One of the sacred twelve he has seduced, possessed and moved to carry out in the most hypocritical, false way his infamous designs. How near he came adding Peter to the black roll of his immortal ones, immortal in infamy, is very evident. That the devil had much every way to do with Peter's dastardly course, his lying and blasphemy, is evident from the words of Christ, "And the Lord said unto Simon, Simon, behold Satan hath desired to have you that he may sift you as wheat. But I have prayed for thee, that thy faith fail not; and when thou art converted, strengthen thy brethren. And he said unto him, Lord, I am ready to go with thee, both into prison, and to death. And he said, I tell thee, Peter, the cock shall not crow this day, before that thou shalt thrice deny that thou knowest me."

In the Parable of the Sower Christ sets forth the unseen but powerful influence which the devil exerts to neutralize the word of God. In the record of this parable by Matthew, the devil is termed the "wicked one," a statement of personality and of the concentration and comprehension of preëminent wickedness. He catches away the word sown with vigilant and diabolical hate. "Then cometh the devil and taketh the word." He is the destroyer of the seeds of good. So powerful is he that the word of God, incorruptible and eternal, is prevented from securing its benign and saving efforts by his vigilance and influence over the mind.

In the story of Job and his sore trials, we see the Sabeans and Chaldeans are ready to respond to his suggestion to make their predatory raids on Job's herds. Satan's power is not limited to outside influence, but is direct and powerful, getting into the inside, and making suggestions of evil, almost godlike sometimes, and again so inflaming our passions or principles that we cannot see the wrong till too late, as in the case of Satan's suggestion to David to number Israel. His power is so great that even good men, the best, who are able to resist his temptations, yet for a time are under his power. The Christians at Smyrna were so under his power that while he could not alienate their affections or disturb their loyalty, he could put them in prison. Paul felt all his life the rankling poison of a wound inflicted by Satan's power.

Peter was in his hands and tossed about, and was brought nigh to the fatal verge by his power. Job was for a while put in his power, and was driven and torn and desolated like a cruel and reckless tempest, wherein everything was wrecked and lost but his patience. How great was Satan's power to destroy fortune and family and friends and reputation! The Son of God was in his mysterious and all desolating power, led to the mountains and led to the temple by the fearful spell of Satan. Angels retired and heaven hushed its music and was draped in silence and trembled in awe while Satan's dread power was allowed to spend its dark force on heaven's Anointed One. The power of disease was in the devil's hands. He smote Job. Christ said of the woman with the spirit of infirmity: "Ought not this woman, being a daughter of Abraham, whom Satan hath bound, lo! these eighteen years, be loosed from this bond on the Sabbath day?" Doubtless much of sickness is due to the power of the devil. To this there is reference in the statements of Christ's work. "When the even was come, they brought unto him many that were possessed with devils; and he cast out the spirits with his word, and healed all that were sick. That it might be fulfilled which was spoken by Isaiah, the prophet, saying, Himself took our infirmities, and bare our sicknesses." " How God anointed Jesus of Nazareth with the Holy Ghost and with power; who went about doing good, and healing all that were oppressed of the devil; for God was with him."

Satan's power did not extend to death in Job's case, but it did in that of his children. The Smyrna Christians he could hold in prison but ten days, but thousands of others he held unto death. His own cruel, deadly hands weaved for them the martyr's crown of gold and glory.

The power of the devil over the body is further seen and illustrated by numbers of cases in the New Testament, of demoniacal possessions. The devil had possession by some of his imps of the bodies of persons. Some of the cases were fearfully tormented in body and almost wrecked in mind, others had functions of the body suspended, some were made dumb by him, and others made deaf and blind. These cases were many in number and of great variety. The great power and malignity of Satan is seen in that among the most distressing cases were those who were not noted for great sins, but the young and comparative innocent ones were the victims of his dread power. The whole person came under the power of this alien spirit.

The power of Satan, his nearness and personality, had a constant and destructive manifestation in these cases.

Of these demoniacal possessions it has been well said that the Gospel narratives are distinctly pledged to the historic truth of these occurrences. Either they are true or the Gospels are false.

Nor can it be said they represent the opinions of the times. They relate to us words spoken by the Lord Jesus in which the personality and presence of the devil are distinctly stated. Now either our Lord spoke these words or He did not. If He did not, then we must at once set aside the concurrent testimony of the Evangelists to a plain matter of fact. In other words, we establish a principle which will overthrow equally every fact related in the Gospels.

X

THE POWER OF THE DEVIL (*Continued*)

Christ's physical sufferings before Pilate; His awful scourging with the Roman thongs; His hanging between heaven and earth by copper nails; His bleeding brow surmounted with a wreath of thorns; were no more severe perhaps than many saints endured upon crosses just after His day, and later in the fires of Smithfield. The inexplicable mental suffering of Christ when God withdrew His face from Him, was the suffering that broke His pure heart. When Christ's physical sufferings were at the climax, then it was that God permitted the soul of Jesus to enter for a few moment's into the soul of death,—the horror a sinner experiences the moment he is adrift from Time and his hope is dead. Jesus could not bear it for a moment and cried: "My God, my God, why hast thou forsaken me?" O! Sinner, O! Sinner, if Christ's heart was broken at the momentary experience of a soul lost eternally, what will you do?—*H. W. Hodge.*

THE power of Satan is far greater than that of God's highest and saintliest earthly ones. In the third chapter of Zechariah we have the picture of his power with God's high official representatives. Joshua, the high priest, is there, the angel of the Lord is there, and standing at Joshua's right to resist all his righteous acts is Satan. Joshua and the angel, realizing their insufficiency when contending with

Satan, they send a cry to heaven, "The Lord rebuke thee, O Satan."

Jude gives us this item. "Michael the archangel, when contending with the devil he disputed about the body of Moses, durst not bring him a railing accusation, but saith, The Lord rebuke thee."

Whatever this obscure text may mean in regard to this contest between Michael and the devil, while it teaches us spirit and tongue control, it does, without obscurity or doubt, clearly show that an archangel's strength is not sufficient to contend single-handed and alone with the devil.

Daniel gives a side glance into the power and conflicts which exist in the unseen and spiritual world which lies so near our own, which has so much to do with us where our spiritual battles are fought, and victories won. Daniel had been praying three weeks before the angel and the answer came. "Then said he unto me, Fear not, Daniel, for from the first day that thou didst set thine heart to understand and to chasten thyself before thy God thy words were heard and I am come for thy words. But the prince of the Kingdom of Persia withstood me one and twenty days; but lo, Michael, one of the chief princes, came to help me." We see how he plans. If he cannot keep people from praying nor absolutely prevent the answer to prayer, he can cause delay in the answer to prayer that he may discourage and break down faith and discount urgent, importunate praying.

He has power to cast into prison. To the little pious church at Smyrna, Jesus Christ writes in commendation, warning and consolation: " Fear none of those things which thou shalt suffer; behold, the devil shall cast some of you into prison, that ye may be tried; and ye shall have tribulation ten days. Be thou faithful unto death, and I will give thee a crown of life."

There are special seats or headquarters of his power, places where the devil makes his home and rules with an absolute sway. To this Christ refers in His letter to the Church of Pergamos: " I know thy works, and where thou dwellest, even where Satan's seat is; and thou holdest fast my name, and hast not denied my faith, even in those days wherein Antipas was my faithful martyr, who was slain among you, where Satan dwelleth."

Some said they were Jews, but were the " synagogue of Satan." Are there churches which are called Christian, but are churches of Satan?

In Christ's letters to the seven Churches in Asia, we see how the ascended and enthroned Son of God presents the same view of the devil. The " depths " of Satan are referred to in the address to Thyatira. In this Revelation of Christ to John, the devil is still declared to be " the great dragon, the old serpent, the devil, and Satan." He is declared to have great " wrath."

The devil's power is greatly and strangely enhanced by his system of worship, which, while it degrades, it fascinates and holds. The system of pagan worship and devotion is very powerful. It holds its devotees by iron chains. It is not a work of chance, neither does it spring from native religious instincts. It is a system of rare power and of rare skill, constructed by a graduate in the craft of seduction and delusion. Satan's hand and head are in it, all planning, ordering, and inspiring it. It is this fact which gives its strength and influence.

Of Jeroboam, who perverted the religious instinct and debased worship for sinister, worldly, and selfish purposes, it is said he ordained him priests for the devils. The Psalmist declared they sacrificed unto devils. The New Testament declares that " the things which the Gentiles sacrifice, they sacrifice to devils, and not to God; and I would not that ye should have fellowship with devils. Ye cannot drink the cup of the Lord and the cup of devils; ye cannot be partakers of the Lord's table and of the table of devils." Again we have it declared, " Now the Spirit speaketh expressly, that in the latter times some shall depart from the faith, giving heed to seducing spirits, and doctrines of devils."

The intensity and power of the devil's worship is illustrated and enforced in the last book of the New Testament, showing how his worship would increase in intensity and would militate against the worship of the Lamb. We have all along rival altars and rival worship. The devil is the author, inspirer, and protector of the one, and Christ is the author, inspirer and protector of the true and pure worship. There are wonders in each, miracles and martyrs in the false and devilish, as well as in the true and heavenly.

Revelation summarizes the situation: "And they had a king over them, which is the angel of the bottomless pit, whose name in the Hebrew tongue is Abaddon, but in the Greek tongue hath his name Apollyon. One woe is past; and, behold, there come two woes more hereafter."

These are not lawless woes, nor are their authors lawless bands, disorderly and reckless mobs. They are organized. The strictest obedience to the devil prevails. "Devil with devil damned firm concord holds." They are "principalities and powers," not only of high and first order in creation, not only of great personal power and dignity, but ordered and sub-ordered, coördinate and subordinate. There is the most perfect government, military in its drill and discipline, absolute and orderly in its arrangement, under one supreme, dictatorial, powerful head, with rank and file and officers complete. "For our wrestling is not against flesh and blood but against principalities, against the powers, against the world, rulers of this darkness, against the spiritual hosts of wickedness in the heavenly places." These high and wicked spirits are every-where. They fill the air, are everywhere intent on evil, following the direction of their leader, carrying out his plans with hearty accord, ready obedience and implicit confidence. How loathsome their nature! How marvellous and miracle-working their power! How high and kingly their influence! How martial their purposes! All this is vividly and strongly set forth in the sixteenth chapter of Revelation: "And I saw Three unclean spirits like frogs come out of the mouth of the dragon, and out of the mouth of the beast, and out of the mouth of the false prophet. For they are the spirits of devils, working miracles, which go forth unto the kings of the earth and of the whole world, to gather them to the battle of that great day of God Almighty."

The power of Satan finds its great increase and expression in the efforts and instrumentality of the unregenerate, who are by Bible teaching under his power, subjects of his kingdom of darkness. More than that, so intimate is their connection with Satan, so close the unity, purpose and relationship, that they belong to his family. His paternity gives birth and character to them, his fatherhood binds them in a strong embrace.

The power of the devil—how defiant, bold, sacrilegious, presumptuous! How near the sacred person of Christ he came! See how he invaded the sacred circle of His chosen apostles. Judas falls from his high position—tempted, possessed by Satan and filled with remorse and infamy, committing suicide, and hell is his forever.   Peter acts as the spokesman of the devil, becomes the advocate of a non-cross bearing, non-self-denying, worldly religion.   He is so affected by the devil's power that he curses and swears and lies, and finds himself all besmirched, bemired and befouled, from which he is only saved by the prayers and look of Christ.   John and James fell a prey to the devil as they wanted fire to come down from heaven and burn up the Samaritans.   Christ sharply shows that they had not His Spirit, but the other spirit, the spirit of the destroyer which actuated them. Paul had his apostolic plans interfered with and hindered by the devil.   To the Thessalonians, he writes: "Wherefore we would have come unto you, even I, Paul, once and again; but Satan hindered us."   And he bore to his grave the marks of the power of this inveterate foe to apostolic fidelity.

The power of Satan is not supreme.   It is limited.   It was so in Job's case.   Satan could go only so far to afflict.   Since the Son of God came into the world, the devil's power has been curtailed. The cross gave a shock to Satan and his power. Death, his realm has been abolished, and "life and immortality brought to light through the gospel." His kingdom received its death stroke on Calvary. The almighty forces of the Gospel are laying hold of the mighty forces of Satan.

XI

THE DEVIL, AND HIS METHODS

Christ fought three notable battles with the Devil and his demons. I am pleased to call them:

1st. The Battle of the Wilderness.

2nd. The Battle of Gethsemane.

3rd. The Battle of Calvary.

In the battle of the wilderness, there were no seconds, and no trench warfare; and in the open, Christ met the three onslaughts of His wily adversary; three times His enemy retreated. The first charge we call *DISTRUST;* that is, Satan suggested: "Leave off a life of dependence on God; take things in your own hand and make these stones bread." Jesus drew the sword of the Spirit up to the hilt in His adversary when He quoted this passage, viz., "Man shall not live by bread alone but by every word that proceedeth out of the mouth of God" (Matt. 4:4).

—*H. W. Hodge.*

BOTH in the New Testament and in the Old, the devil is represented as being most assiduous and tireless in his activities and efforts. In Job, in answer to God's inquiry, "Whence comest thou?" he replies, "From going to and fro in the earth, and from walking up and down in it." The declaration is one of rapid and extensive goings and of repeated and careful observation. In Peter he is said to be "walking about as a roaring lion." Activity, scrutiny, power and purpose are in his methods.

Thomas à Kempis says: " Know that the ancient enemy doth strive by all means to hinder thy desire to be good and to keep thee clear of all religious exercises.   Many evil thoughts does he suggest to thee, that so he may cause a weariness and horror in thee, and to call thee back from prayer and holy reading."

The careless and half-hearted Christian knows nothing of the devil or his devices, but the souls astir for God and the good, on a stretch for heaven, they are the ones who demand his attention, provoke his ire and call forth his machinations.

Says that marvellous man of faith and power, Pastor Blumhart: " He who is ignorant of the wiles and artifices of the enemy, only beats the air, and the devil is not afraid of him."   Blumhart himself is an illustration.   " In interesting myself in behalf of one possessed," he says, " I became involved in such a fearful conflict with the powers of darkness as is not possible for me to describe."

Christians may live and die all unaware of the devil's being and hate, and he may be as indifferent to their religion because they are unharmful of his kingdom.   But wherever one of the Blumhart type lives, there is a big commotion and fear in Satan's realm.

Satan works by imitation.   To make something as near like the true as possible, and thereby break the force and value of the genuine.   This is one of his favourite methods.   As Jannes and Jambres withstood Moses by their false tricks, so is he carrying on by lying wonders his work. As his apostles are transformed into angels of light, so his wonders are looked on as first class miracles. They do indeed discount true miracles.

What of the revelations of his person? God and Christ have been revealed to men in bodily shape, by figure, by representation. Matchless, majestic, beatific theophanies have holy men seen of God. Has the devil power to clothe himself in form and object to the eye? Can he incarnate himself? He seems to have clothed himself in some visible shape at the temptation of Christ. The form is not recorded. Perhaps in that of a man, doubtless a pious man, gathering in the assembly of the righteous, or as a pious hermit in the seclusion and retirement of the desert. In the days of Christ he revealed himself by taking absolute possession and sway over the person, and used other personalities through which to manifest his being and power. His manifestations are disguises, insidious and deceptive. Sometimes as " an angel of light," with the bloom, beauty, and spices of paradise on him. His person unearthly in splendour, his voice gentle, musical, winning, with no lines or traces of the fall.

The devil affects the body, and through the body affects loyalty to Christ. Job was tried by his sickness. So the devil tries us by sickness. In the days of Christ, he carried on a large business by affecting the body, not simply by ordinary diseases, but by what is termed, "possessed with a devil." In those cases his work was by breaking down the body in some of its chief functions.

His method is to assume that shape which will suit his purposes at the time. Doubtless there was something in the shape or character of the serpent which gave him the readier access to Eve. Garbed as an angel of light his appearance commends him fully to the pure and unsuspecting. As a thorn he desires to give only pain to those who, like Paul, cannot be seduced nor swerved from the fixed course of fidelity. The Christians at Smyrna he puts in prison that by that process he may fetter their bodies whose souls he could not fetter. With matchless cunning and unspeakable fidelity he plies his trade to seduce and damn.

He has access to the minds of men from which he ought forever to be barred. But he has so much of diabolical trickery that he clothes the meanest act with the fairest guise, and conceals a world of infamy with beautiful rainbow colourings. He hoodwinked good David and provoked him to number Israel in opposition to God's will, and brought swift and fearful judgment on the nation.

He readily snatches away from the mind the truth which is superficially received. He also blinds the minds of them which believe not and obstructs the light of saving truth. His process of taking the word out of the heart to prevent faith, and of blinding the mind to the beauties and light of salvation, is a very common one with him.

He makes people sick for the same end as he did Job. He entices men to do wrong, and inflames and urges them on to evil. He keeps at it and eats no idle bread. He takes the Word of God out of the untilled heart and sows tares among the wheat. The devil goes out into the wilderness, finds us in a fainting, discouraged condition, the pulsations of faith weak, its sky cloudy and its vision misty. Then he shows us the world from the loftiest peak of observation, apparelled in its most attractive form, and tries to ensnare us by its bewildering glories. He never tires in trying to ruin us till the coffin lid is on our folded arms and closed eyes, and our happy spirits are bathing in the land "where the wicked cease from troubling and the weary are at rest." With the wisdom of an archangel and the observation and experience of half an eternity, as the Captain General of all the hosts of hell, he is an adept in the acts and arts of deception and trickery, and has almost exhaustless resources at command to serve his purposes. A wiser and more powerful spirit than Satan (save God) perhaps does not live, a more malignant one than he could not be. There is no greater worker than he. His inveterate industry and tireless perseverance are the only things in him worthy of imitation. There are in him the things that make him so potent and so dreadful.

In the Parable of the Sower, we are taught the devil's ability to work on the mind, and take away the good impression there made. "And those by the wayside are they that have heard; then cometh the devil, and taketh away the word from their heart, that they may not believe and be saved." We are also taught how the devil influences the mind to do the most dastardly things, in the case of Judas, chosen as an apostle, into high and holy fellowship, a royal vocation, a select company. Satan had much to do in influencing Judas to the great crime that brought him to despair and suicide, and to immortal infamy in this world and hell in the next.

Satan's thorn in the flesh changed Paul's sorrow into joys, his poverty into wealth, his weakness into strength, his reproaches into sweet heavenly solaces. So mightily does God work to make Satan's all bad work together for good to the faithful ones. As an old saint says, " The devil is but a whetstone to sharpen the faith and patience of the saints." He may keep God busy polishing the stones which he makes rough, but the devil's dirt makes their luster brighter, and they become genuine diamonds of first water.

His methods are as varied as the men with whom he deals. The devil knows man, and that which is much more, he knows men.

To Eve he came in the guise of a well-wisher, subtle, serpentine, and deadly, behind the guise,

He incites her to disobedience by pointing her to higher heights of godlikeness, along paths of sensual and animal enjoyment. A fearful charge of the false and selfish is lodged in her mind against God. No malignity is seen, no distress or anguish does he use. He allures, deceives, ensnares.

How striking the contrast in his method with Job. A man, by God's own estimate, of divinest mould, " None like him in the earth, a perfect and an upright man, one that feareth God and escheweth evil." What methods can he devise for this the saintliest of the saints? He begins by accusing him to God as selfish in his motives, reducing his piety to the worldly, selfish and sinister. No alluring paths, no divergent flowery ways are pointed out to Job, not a word is said to him. With not a premonition, without a note of warning, as an awful surprise and shock, at one fell and desolating blow, his family of ten children are dead, his princely fortune gone, and one dark hour has bereft him of family and fortune. Stripped naked by the fearful rapidity and depth of his losses, he becomes homeless, childless and friendless, in a grief inconsolable, and a pall of mystery impenetrable and insoluble.

The integrity of Job, like a column blackened by the smoke, but unrent and unshaken by the fiery ordeal, is still pursued by the devil. Still he insinuates and charges the genuineness of Job's piety. He sees nothing of noble fidelity, of lofty loyalty in

Job. He still attributes low motives as the basis of his integrity. No touch of sympathy, no relentings, with heartless cruelty and malignity, he pursues his death-dealing work. Out of his magazine of hellish enginery he comes with a loathsome disease. He concenters on this one saint, woe after woe, and affliction upon affliction, till his wife is alienated, his friends estranged, his enemies triumphant. His hopeless, bitter grief has not one ingredient to relieve, his pious reputation blackening, his body tortured, his mind in agony. This is one method of Satan's to distress and defame those whom he cannot seduce.

To the Son of God in the wilderness, he comes not as he did to Job in lowering and seething storms of distress, but in the form of apparent sympathy and friendliness. It may have been in the guise of a saintly hermit in the wilderness. " If thou be the Son of God "—you want this matter of your sonship to God settled, and so do I. You are very hungry and faint. " Command that these stones be made bread." An innocent and a proper way to settle at once a great question and to appease a great hunger.

Then he comes to Christ with the sanctity of the holiest place, and affords Him an opportunity to attest before the wondering and awe-struck worshippers His Messiahship, a shorter and a better road this to gain credence to His mission than the slow and thankless process of daily teaching and daily ministering, and marching to the cross with the dark shadows of its shame and heaviness ever darkening His way.

Satan's desperate venture was to seduce Him by the world's array of grandeur, power and glory. Satan plunged Job from serene and cloudless, heavenly height down to a midnight, starless and stormy. To the Son of God he would be a present friend to save Him from pain, poverty, hunger, shame, toil and death.

XII

THE DEVIL AND HIS METHODS
(*Continued*)

The battle of Gethsemane opened on Thursday night in an upper room in Jerusalem. It commenced by one-twelfth of Christ's body guard being captured by a bribe of twenty dollars. The real battle opened Thursday evening near midnight. He set Peter, James and John on picket duty inside the garden in a stone's throw of His redoubt; the eight disciples He commissioned as the outer watch. The battle of Gethsemane was fierce when Jesus fell on His face and prayed saying, "O, my Father, if it be possible, let this cup pass from me; nevertheless, not as I will but as thou wilt." Jesus then summoned His human reinforcements, but alas, "Human sympathy is comforting but helpless." The second time amid legions of Devils and the curse of a world's sin, He sought His body guard; the second time they were asleep. But Jesus won. "And there appeared an angel unto him from heaven, strengthening him." The angel took Jesus in his arms and wiped the death sweat and blood from His face and comforted Him. This is one time it seems He was made "A little lower than the angels." The second battle completed; the Devil defeated.

—*H. W. Hodge.*

THE devil is rarely seen in his movements and methods. He has rare tact in getting others to do his work and execute his plans.

His methods are to blind, to put a veil on the evil results and all the sad consequences of sin. He so blinds that the evil cannot be seen. So with the keen-eyed David, brave, true and clear-eyed for God, yet Satan blinded him completely to the treachery, infamy and murder in Uriah's case. So sinners are held by him in unbelief. He puts out their eyes to all the light and glory of the Shining Sun of Righteousness. " In whom the god of this world hath blinded the minds of them which believe not, lest the light of the glorious gospel of Christ, who is the image of God, should shine unto them."

The power of the devil extends to the mind. He can influence the mind, insinuate thoughts, suggest purposes, excite the imagination, inflame the passions, stir the appetites, kindle the fleshy fires, awaken old habits, and fan old dead flames or light new ones. The artless purity of Eve he beguiled. He entered into the half traitorous Judas and possessed him fully, and made his half-formed treason full and his treachery immortal in its infancy. He was in the private council of Ananias and Sapphira, a party of their fraud, and suggested their lying plan to deceive the apostles. His access to the mind is evident in that he snatches away the divine seed implanted by holy lips in the soil of the heart as taught in the Parable of the Sower.

In Corinthians the devil is called " the god of this world." " The god of this world hath blinded the minds of them which believe not, lest the light of the glorious gospel of Christ, who is the image of God, should shine unto them."

The devil uses this world as a veil to shut out the truth of God, the light of His glorious Gospel, and to close the eyes of faith to all the discoveries in the unseen and eternal.

The antagonism between the children of the world possessed by Satan, and the children of God possessed by God, is set forth by John. " Ye are of God, little children, and have overcome them; because greater is he that is in you, than he that is in the world. They are of the world; therefore speak they of the world, and the world heareth them. We are of God; he that knoweth God heareth us; he that is not of God heareth not us. Hereby know we the spirit of truth and the spirit of error."

Who is in us? God. Who is in the children of the world? The devil. Our faith, our hope and our final triumph are in the truth of the Word of God. " Greater is he that is in us than he that is in the world."

Satan perverts the things which are truly works of God and misemploys miracles to obscure God's glory.

The devil often tries to break the soul down and reduce it to despair. He tells us to discourage us that we shall never succeed. The way is too hard and narrow and the burden too heavy.

He takes advantage of weak and distracted nerves, and suggests fears. Grace is hid from the sight, shortcomings are magnified and infirmities are classed as gross sins. Sometimes the fear of death is used by Satan to quench the fire of faith, and the grave becomes something awful. He darkens the future. Heaven and God will be out of sight, hidden by a thick veil of to-morrow's cares, trials and needs. The imaginary disasters, failures and evils of to-morrow are powerful weapons in Satan's hand. He suggests that the Lord is a hard master, and that His promises will fail. He works on the remaining corruption in the heart, and raises a great storm in the soul.

Samuel Rutherford says:—"Oh, if our faith could ride out against the high and proud waves and winds when our sea seemeth all on fire! Oh, how oft do I let my grips go. I am put to swimming and half sinking. I find the devil hath the advantage of the ground in this battle, for he fighteth in known ground in our corruption. However matters go, it is our happiness to win new grounds daily in Christ's love, and to purchase a new piece of it daily, and to add conquest to conquest, till our Lord Jesus and we be so near each other that Satan shall not draw a straw or a thread betwixt us."

He tempts to evil tempers, to hasty words, to impatience and to carnal reasoning, which is his powerful ally in our minds. Back to Christ. More of His Spirit-renewed and thorough self-dedication, and in darting prayers upward by an uplifted eye and heart—thus will we be able to resist and conquer the great adversary of our souls.

One of the most intelligent and God-honoured among the saintliest of saints wrote: " I have keen inward sufferings, what are termed the buffetings of Satan. Horror at times has taken hold of me. I felt much, but feared more."

The devil may tempt us to think too meanly of ourselves as Moses did, and too highly of ourselves as Peter did. In one sense, we cannot think too meanly of ourselves, but in another we can. He persuades us that we are so poor and weak we can do nothing, and so we are weakened in faith and broken in effort. But his master method is to fill us with self, self-importance and self-ability, and then not only is faith weakened, but destroyed. Our efforts and doings may increase in number and vain show, but the seal of self and Satan are on them all.

John Wesley notes: " I preached at eight on that delicate device of Satan to destroy the whole religion of the heart. The telling Christians not to regard frames or feelings, but to live by naked faith, is in plain terms, not to regard either love, joy, peace or any other fruit of the Spirit; not to regard whether they feel them or the reverse; whether their souls be in a heavenly or hellish frame. Satan's method with some is to make them rely too much on frames and feelings. With others he deals the reverse and urges them to discard all frames and feelings."

Many anxious errors sprang up with the rank

growth in Wesley's day, and he pruned and trimmed with a master's hand. Naked faith is often nothing but a sapless, arid, fruitless, unconscious thing, and brings an arid, fruitless, unconscious salvation with it, if it brings salvation at all.

Whatever may be his method, how numberless his devices, the words of his conqueror to us are these: " Behold, I give unto you power to tread on serpents and scorpions, and over all the power of the enemy; and nothing shall by any means hurt you." Of this text, Miss Havergal writes: " Why, this is grand—*power over all the power* of the enemy. Just where he is strongest there they shall prevail. Not over the very center of his power, not over his power here and there, nor now and then, but over *all* his power. And Jesus said, Is not that enough to go into battle with? "

The devil's brain is prolific in plans. He has many ways of doing many things. Perhaps he has many ways of doing each thing. With him nothing is stereotyped. He never runs in ruts. Fruitful, diverse and ever fresh, is his way of doing things. Indirect, disingenuous, insidious and graceful are his plans. He acts by artifice and always by guile.

His plans by Bible statement are " wiles." The original word means to follow up or investigate by method and settled plan. It is not a bad word but one of order, arrangement and methods, conceived and executed. But when the word gets into the devil's hand it is defined by his dictionary. It receives a strong tincture, a deep colouring of cunning and trickery.

Sometimes Satan comes disrobed of his heavenly garments, a thorn, sharp and pointed and painful, a poisoned thorn, a thorn that rankles and stays, a thorn that cannot be extracted by prayer, which retrieves all other ills. The saints who have seen most of heaven are often decreed to see most of hell. Saints who have the fullest and most transporting revelation of God, often have the saddest experience of Satan.

Paul's thorn was as much to Paul as his abundance of revelations. His thorn made him more a saint than his vision of the third heavens. Satan only lifted him higher by keeping him lower.

Satan may come to us in his own native character, the thorn breeder and piercer. He may put in us thorns which no prayer power can extract. Thorns which will poison and pain, but the thorn will enrich grace, increase and mature humility and make infirmities strong and glorious. Satan's thorns will clothe necessities with richest attire, change distresses and persecutions into divinest pleasures, make room for God's greatest power in us and on us, make the lowest point of spiritual depression the highest point of vision, and make strength out of weakness and wealth out of poverty.

XIII

EXPOSED POSITIONS

The battle of Calvary: The conflict of Gethsemane closed around the first hour of the fourth watch and the last conflict began immediately in an offensive personal encounter between one of the awakened body guard of Jesus and a servant of Caiaphas. The battle went on with heat and vigour when the High Priest asked Jesus, "Art Thou the Christ, the Son of the Blessed?" And Jesus said, "I am and ye shall see the Son of Man sitting on the right hand of power and coming in the clouds of Heaven." The cross is reached. Though pressed on all sides by Hell, Death and Demons, He provided for His mother. At 2:59 P. M., April 7th He seemed to have lost the battle and said, "Father into Thy hands I commend my spirit. It is finished." He conquered Satan by seeming weakness. He gained the battle of Calvary by a surrender of His life. This is Scriptural. "Through death he deposed him who had the power of death and delivered them who through fear of death were all their lifetime subject to bondage."—*H. W. Hodge.*

THERE are positions and conditions which lie open to the attacks of Satan. These points must be guarded by sleepless vigilance. The devil is a remorseless, cruel and mighty foe. To watch him with unsleeping eye, is not only a duty, but safety to life, deliverance from hell, certainty of heaven, all, and more, if more there can be, are involved in overcoming the devil. Stupidity, neglect, being off guard in the conflict, with

Satan are much more than mistakes or indiscretions. They are fatal undoings, eternal and remediless losses.

The apostle places his Corinthian brethren on the vantage ground in the war with the devil by declaring, " We are not ignorant of Satan's devices." Ignorance is always an exposed condition. Ignorance is open to attack and surprise by day and by night. To be ignorant of the existence, character and ways of the devil, is the prelude and prophecy of fatal results in the fight for heaven. If this be true, how hopeless is the case of one who is not only ignorant of the temptations, but denies or ignores the existence of the tempter. The devil's great device, his masterpiece of temptation, is to destroy faith in his own existence. God's struggle is to establish faith. The devil's great work is to eradicate all spiritual facts, principles and persons, good or evil, God and devil. He who denies or ignores the existence of the devil, puts a fatal bar to ultimate salvation, paralyzes all efforts in that direction, and gives one over, chained hand and foot, to the merciless foe whose existence has been denied and derided. Nothing advances Satan's work with more skilful and readier hands than to be ignorant of Satan and his ways. To escape his snare, we must not only have a strong faith in the fact that Satan is, but also must have a most intimate knowledge of him and of his plans and many-sided ways.

Much akin to the foregoing exposed position is the one which makes light of Satan. Frivolous views of him, his works, or his character, light talk or dishonouring epithets in the line of jesting—are all detrimental to any serious views of life's great work, its solemn engagements, its serious conflicts and its weighty hindrances. Presumption, self-will and foolishness are the characteristics of those who thus deal with these weighty concernments. The existence and work of the devil is a serious matter, and it is to be considered and dealt with from the most serious standpoint, and none but serious people can deal with it. And with this well accords the iterated and reiterated New Testament exhortation and note of warning, "be sober." That which gives it point and arousing power is, "Be sober, for your adversary, the devil," etc.

How germane to this attitude is Jude's nervous, incisive, and almost rough handling of these sacrilegious characters, who make light of sacred things and sacred persons.

"Likewise also, these filthy dreamers defile the flesh, despise dominion, and speak evil of dignities. Yet Michael the archangel, when contending with the devil, he disputed about the body of Moses, durst not bring against him a railing accusation, but said, The Lord rebuke thee. But these speak evil of those things which they know not; but what they know naturally, as brute beasts, in those things they corrupt themselves."

Peter takes the same class of flippant irreverent talkers to task somewhat after the same manner: " Presumptuous are they, self-willed, they are not afraid to speak evil of dignities. Whereas angels, which are greater in power and might, bring not railing accusation against them before the Lord. But these, as natural brute beasts made to be taken and destroyed, speak evil of the things that they understand not, and shall utterly perish in their own corruption; and shall receive the reward of unrighteousness, as they that count it pleasure to riot in the daytime. Spots they are and blemishes, sporting themselves with their own deceivings while they feast with you."

A paralyzing attitude, a staying to talk, a listening to Satan's insinuations, are all fatal. This was Eve's mistake. His tongue is smooth as oil, his words circulate and inflame like poison. Bristling opposition, embattled for war, no inlets, no down bars, no open gates, no low places; all fenced, and high, and shut against the devil, is the only safety.

An unforgiving spirit invites Satanic possession. His favourite realm is the spirit. To corrupt that, to incense or provoke to retaliation, revenge or unmercifulness—that is his chosen work and his most common and successful device. Paul puts it to the front so as to thwart Satan: " To whom ye forgive anything, I forgive also; for if I forgive anything, to whom I forgive it, for your sakes forgive I it in the person of Christ; lest Satan should get an advantage of us; for we are not ignorant of his devices."

When he begets an unforgiving spirit in us, then he has us, we are on his ground. Then wicked men and good men, all kinds of men, are likely to do us harm, sometimes at vital and very sensitive points. Sometimes all unconsciously they wrong us and sometimes knowingly and wilfully they wrong us. As soon as a spirit of unkindness possesses us for the wrong done, Satan has the upper hand.

We quote from the Revised Version the warning words of our Saviour: " Again, ye have heard that it hath been said by them of old time, Thou shalt not forswear thyself, but shall perform unto the Lord thine oaths. But I say unto you, Swear not at all; neither by heaven, for it is God's throne; nor by the earth, for it is his footstool; neither by Jerusalem, for it is the city of the great king. Neither shalt thou swear by thy head, because thou canst not make one hair white or black. But let your communication be, yea, yea; nay, nay; for whatsoever is more than these cometh of the evil one." The injunction is against strong oaths in language. Expletives and appeals and declarings added to our words all are wrong, and expose us to the snare of Satan. " In the multitude of words," says Proverbs, "there wanteth not sin."

Satan tempts us to asseverations and declarations to confirm truth which destroy truth. Equivocal words and words by way of substantiating the truth of those already spoken, expose us to Satan's power. "But above all things, my brethren, swear not, neither by heaven, neither by the earth, neither by any other oath; but let your yea, be yea; and your nay, nay; lest ye fall into condemnation." So St. James seals the words of Christ. The devil lies concealed in many words. Simplicity, fewness and seriousness of words, mightily hinder and thwart his ensnaring plans.

It is so easy for the devil to stop us just a little short of a faith that will save. There are many initials, prefaces, preludes and introductions which are sometimes quite taxing, and are a right good advance in the right direction, but which do not bring us into the heart of the matter. Like Sarah they start with full intent to go to Canaan, but stop at Haran and dwell there. Like Jacob, Shechem stays their steps and holds them instead of Bethel.

On the other hand, even those who are earnestly striving after that "holiness without which no man shall see the Lord," Satan tempts them to go a little too far and their zeal degenerates into party spirit and unhallowed heat. "Strict earnestness degenerates into severity, gentleness into weakness, energetic activity into imprudent meddling and narrowness, calm moderation into careless acquiescence, bold decision maintaining its own convictions firmly becomes intolerant, self-opinionated, narrow, arbitrary, bigoted. Due regard for the peculiarities and convictions of others degenerates into paralyzing indifference and skeptical indolence. Lively trust lapses into presumption and haughtiness, a wise prudence into cowardice and hesitating anxiety," and confession and profession degenerate into and evaporate into aridity. So Satan watches and is alert always, and wary, to hold us back from the goal, or to press us by an impetuous, unkindly or vehement spirit to go beyond the goal. So all this uncovers often our strongest positions and turns them into exposed conditions.

Yoking with unbelievers in the relationship of life-ties of friendship and intimate and confiding associations with unbelievers, are exposed positions of great peril, and of which the devil takes instant and great advantage. Partnership in business, or the more sacred relation of marriage with unbelievers, is perilous to one united to Christ by close ties.

Satan is called Belial by the apostle, meaning worthlessness, contemptibleness, wickedness. He and Christ cannot be joined in agreement. No unequal yoking, no fellowship, no communion, no concord, no agreement can exist. All is perilous and mixed. Contamination and impurity result. A maimed enfeebled holiness is the fruit of these voluntary close yokings. Under the law, an ox and an ass could not be yoked together. Under the Spirit, Christ and Satan can have no concord.

Separation, cleansing and perfected holiness are necessary to secure the vantage ground against Satan. How strong, minute, explicit, and comprehensive, is the charge here given against union, communion or intimate association with unbelievers. Unequally yoked, no pulling together, not equal, no fellowship, no sharing, no communion, no intimacy, no concord, no agreement, no part, no portion, no agreement, no voting together. Commentators have found in this great variety of expression, Paul's fine command of the Greek language. We find in it the fire of impassioned and profound convictions, demanding the most self-denying abstemiousness in forming intimate and voluntary associations with the unbelieving world in the way of business and pleasurable or social pursuits and intimacies.

This rule he laid down in his first epistle to the Corinthians: " I wrote unto you in an epistle not to company with fornicators. Yet not altogether with the fornicators of this world, or with the covetous, or extortioners, or with idolaters; for then must ye needs go out of the world. But now I have written unto you not to keep company, if any man that is called a brother be a fornicator, or covetous, or an idolater, or a railer, or a drunkard, or an extortioner; with such a one, no, not to eat." Not the casual, courteous Christian intercourse, was he objecting to and barring, but the more intimate, voluntary and social.

St. James locates and defines and opposes these affinities and attachments as not only "exposed positions," but resulting in the most radical and criminal violation of the holiest relationship.   I quote from the Revised Version: "Ye adulteresses, know ye not that the friendship of the world is enmity with God? Whosoever, therefore, would be a friend of the world maketh himself an enemy of God."   By it the marriage vow of God is broken.

Dean Alford, commenting on this passage, says: "Of the world, it means men and men's interest, ambitions and employments, in so far as they are without God. The man who is taken out of the world by Christ cannot again become the friend and companion of worldly men and their schemes for self, without passing into enmity with God. God and the world stand opposed to one another, so that a man cannot join the one without deserting the other. He, therefore, who is minded to be the friend of the world, and sets his mind and thought and wish that way, must make up his mind to be God's enemy."

"But must I not be intimate with my relations, and that whether they fear God or not? Has not His providence recommended these to me?" Undoubtedly it has, but there are relations nearer or more distant. The nearest relations are husbands and wives. As these have taken each other for better or worse, they must make the best of each other, seeing as God has joined them together,

none can put them asunder, unless in case of
adultery, or when the life of one or the other is in
imminent danger.   Parents are almost as nearly
connected with their children.   You cannot part
with them while they are young, it being your duty
to "train them up," with all care, "in the way
wherein they should go."   How frequently you
should converse with them when they are grown
up, is to be determined by Christian prudence.
This also will determine how long it is expedient
for children, if it be at their own choice, to remain
with their parents.   In general, if they do not fear
God, you should leave them as soon as is convenient.   As for all other relations, even brothers
or sisters, if they are of the world, you are under
no obligation to be intimate with them.   You may
be civil and friendly at a distance.

But allowing that "the friendship of the world
is enmity against God," and consequently, that it
is the most excellent way, indeed the only way to
heaven, to avoid all intimacy with worldly men,
yet, who has resolution to walk therein? who even
of those that love or fear God?   Whatever it cost
thee, flee spiritual adultery!   Have no friendship
with the world.   However tempted thereto by
profit or pleasure, contract no intimacy with
worldly-minded men.   And if thou hast contracted
any such already, break it off without delay.   Yea,
if thy ungodly friend be dear to thee as a right
eye, or useful as a right hand, yet confer not with

flesh and blood, but pluck out the right eye, cut off the right hand, and cast them from thee! It is not an indifferent thing. Thy life is at stake; eternal life or eternal death. And is it not better to go into life having one eye or one hand, than having both, to be cast into hell-fire? However importuned or tempted thereto, have no friendship with the world. Look around, and see the melancholy effects it has produced among your brethren! How many of the mighty have fallen by this very thing! They would take no warning. They would converse, and that intimately, with worldly-minded men, till they "measured back their steps to earth again!" Oh, "come out from among them!" from all unholy men, however harmless they may appear, "and be ye separate," at least, so far as to have no intimacy with them. As your "fellowship is with the Father, and with his Son Jesus Christ," so let it be with those, and those only, who at least seek the Lord Jesus Christ in sincerity. So "shall ye be," in a peculiar sense, "my sons and my daughters, saith the Lord Almighty."

How Satan surrounds us! How strongly he holds us! How he entangles, enchains and fetters us by the worldly association! We lie in the sweet friendship, the embraces and converse of these worldly ones, while they with the whole world lie in the arms of the wicked one.

If simplicity drops out of our faith, our fortications against Satan are weakened. "I am jealous over you with godly jealousy, for I have espoused you to one husband, that I may present you as a chaste virgin to Christ. But I fear, lest by any means as the serpent beguiled Eve through his subtility, so your minds should be corrupted from the simplicity that is in Christ." Here we have Satan recognized in the serpent and his ability in allusion to fall in Eden and intimations that he is still busy at his old tricky trade. Satan has such a dexterous and successful hand at deception that Paul was uneasy. The lack of simplicity would be fatal to their purity and faith, as the taste of the forbidden fruit was fatal to Eve, to her purity and obedience, and to paradise. The loss of a little thing, but with it, all is lost.

An untrained body exposes readily to Satan's assaults. Even the natural, innocent appetites and passions have to be held in with bit and bridle. An apostle was aware of this: " But I keep under my body, and bring it into subjection, lest that by any means, when I have preached to others, I myself should be a castaway." An undisciplined body would hurl Paul from the apostolic heights down to the fearful abyss of apostasy. Two statements are made as to his body. "Keep under" and "bring it into subjection." The first means that part of the face under the eyes. A blow on that part of the face, a black and blue spot by the bruise of a heavy blow, restrained and suppressed by heavy blows, and its native power is broken.

The second statement means to make a slave of, to treat with severity, to subject to stern and rigid discipline. The apostle sets forth the body as an important fact in the contest for heaven, and teaches us that if it be untrained, without the strong repressing, moulding hand of discipline, it becomes an easy prey to the assaults of Satan.

After the same order is the direction of Peter: "Be sober, be vigilant; because your adversary, the devil, as a roaring lion, walketh about, seeking whom he may devour. Whom resist steadfast in the faith, knowing that the same afflictions are accomplished in your brethren that are in the world." A listless, drowsy, sleepy, stupid state, gives us into Satan's power without a struggle or even a surrender, or the decency of a parley.

To the same end is the strong injunction of Christ to the drowsy and fainting disciples: "Watch and pray, that ye enter not into temptation. The spirit indeed is willing, but the flesh is weak."

XIV

EXPOSED POSITIONS (*Continued*)

> My soul, be on thy guard;
>   Ten thousand foes arise:
> The hosts of sin are pressing hard
>   To draw thee from the skies.
>
> O watch, and fight, and pray;
>   The battle ne'er give o'er;
> Renew it boldly every day,
>   And help divine implore.

WE have two statements in first Timothy of serious import in regard to the appointing of men to active and official leadership in the Church. The first is against appointing novices to such leadership. "Not a novice, lest being lifted up with pride, he fall into the condemnation of the devil." To press young converts to the front, to put immature ones into spiritual leadership, is to blind and puff with pride. It is to put the young convert in an exposed place, where he readily falls into the condemnation, into which the devil fell through the blinding effects of pride. This is a text, which by its reminiscential reference, is of much value, giving, as it does, credence to the Church's almost universally received opinion, that the devil fell through pride, its aspiring and blinding and blasting effects. Let the novitiates be hardened and matured by discipline ere they are put to the front. Staying behind is often a greater cross, as well as a greater virtue, than pushing or being pushed to the front. It is always an unsafe place for faith till faith has its beard or grows its spurs.

Men of questionable reputation placed in church leadership or official position, bring reproach and help the devil much in his disgraceful business. " Moreover he must have a good report of them which are without, lest he fall into reproach and the snare of the devil." Men of good character and spotless reputation in the lead of church affairs, closes Satan's mouth, cuts off his revenue, and brings his business low. The violation of these two rules in church control, novices in lead and men whose reputation is not spotless as leaders, puts the novices in bad case, and increases the bad odour of the leaders of questionable repute. The entire Church is also put in an exposed condition, imperilling the whole army. Leaders are standard bearers, conspicuous. They ought to be conspicuous in spotless piety. They ought to be mature in age, sound and advanced in faith and love and sobriety. Gifted, wise, sober, grave, blameless leaders, will make the Church strong and victorious in the day of battle.

Novices in leadership is an exposed condition. Put novices to the rear till sheltered and trained.

Bad reputation is a treacherous or cowardly leadership for God's army.

Young widowhood in sable sadness is an exposed condition. No widower has as keen an eye to invade the sanctities of widowed grief as Satan. Paul writes plainly. He knew the hidden gins of Satan. He writes broadly, tenderly, honestly, with discrimination: " Honour widows that are widows indeed. But if any widow have children or nephews, let them learn first to shew piety at home, and to requite their parents, for that is good and acceptable before God. Now she that is a widow indeed, and desolate, trusteth in God, and continueth in supplications and prayers night and day. But she that liveth in pleasure, is dead while she liveth. But the young widows refuse: for when they have begun to wax wanton against Christ, they will marry, having damnation, because they have cast off their first faith. And withal they learn to be idle, wandering about from house to house; and not only idle, but tattlers also and busybodies, speaking things which they ought not. I will, therefore, that the younger widows marry, bear children, guide the house, give none occasion to the adversary to speak reproachfully. For some are already turned aside after Satan."

This salutary advice relieves the sorrow of the young woman, and puts her where her heart and hands are full of sweet and sacred responsibilities, and nerve, and time, and heart are full of taxing toil. Satan has a hard job to work on a person thus filled fully in heart and hands with holy toil, rearing the home and state and Church of the future.

There are in man what the Scriptures term *lust*, strong natural desires. They are called "lusts of the flesh," "lusts of the eye," "worldly lusts," the "lusts of men." There are things of time and sense which the heart naturally craves after and clamours for. They form the basis of temptation within. A wily and powerful seducer may tempt and lead innocence and purity astray when there is no inward response to his allurements, but these lusts or desires within form the basis and afford the groundwork for Satan's insidious temptations. St. James describes the whole process: "Let no man say when he is tempted, I am tempted of God, for God cannot be tempted with evil, neither tempteth he any man. But every man is tempted, when he is drawn away of his own lusts, and enticed. Then when lust hath conceived, it bringeth forth sin; and sin, when it is finished, bringeth forth death." The term "drawn away" means to "lure forth." The metaphor is from hunting or fishing. As game is lured from its many ranges, so man by lust is allured from the safety of self-restraint to sin. The word "enticed" means a bait, to catch by bait.

The Scriptures demand that these lusts or desires be banned and reprobated.

We see how Satan and the world are in these lusts. The Gospel is a training school in which these lusts are to be denied. "For the grace of God that bringeth salvation hath appeared to all men, teaching us that, denying ungodliness and worldly lusts, we should live soberly, righteously, and godly in this present world." The solemn declaration is made without qualification or deception, a declarative carrying the force of an imperative demand and also that of a condition: "And they that are Christ's have crucified the flesh with the affections and lusts." The whole work of Christ is presented as an engaging and exciting pattern for us to copy in destroying these lusts: "For as much then as Christ hath suffered for us in the flesh, arm yourselves likewise with the same mind; for he that hath suffered in the flesh hath ceased from sin; that he no longer should live the rest of his time in the flesh to the lusts of men, but to the will of God."

We are taught that these lusts are put in opposition to the will of God. They cannot be yielded to and obey God. No man can serve these two masters. These lusts are the basis and sources of corruption. They war against the soul. We are to "put off concerning the former conversation the old man, which is corrupt according to the deceitful lusts; and be renewed in the spirit of your mind, that ye put on the new man, which after God is created in righteousness and true holiness."

The war with Satan is much concerned about these lusts. These lustings after the things of time and sense are not wholly destroyed when we are converted to Christ. They are broken in power, enfeebled more or less, but the remains, the roots of these, are there. Like a tree in life, cut down at its stump, they throw up many shoots. If we allow these shoots to remain they will keep Satan in his work.

They who are content to leave the remains of these lusts in them will be hampered by internal conditions. To allow sin or the tendency to sin to remain in us, is as fatal as the leaving of the remains of the original natives in the land of Canaan was fatal to the piety, peace and prosperity of Israel. God's command to Israel was that those nations were to be destroyed completely so as to leave neither root nor branch. Israel's failure to do this was the source of untold evil to them. Exposed conditions these remaining lusts are, as much so as the remains of a decayed and broken tooth are the exposed conditions of toothache or neuralgia. So we are charged, "For if ye live after the flesh ye shall die; but if ye through the Spirit do mortify the deeds of the body, ye shall live."

In another text we have these words: "They that are Christ's have crucified the flesh, with its affections and lusts." "Lust" is the larger word in Scripture, including the whole world of active lusts and desires. The "affections" is not so much the soul's disease in its more active operations, as the diseased conditions out of which these spring. The lusts spring from the passions and are nourished by them. They deserve the same punishment as the flesh. All, the flesh, the lusts, and affections, are crucified. This puts the Christian in the best fortified condition to resist the attacks of the devil. With these lusts remaining, he is but half armed and wholly exposed.

Low aims in the spiritual life, satisfaction and quiescence in present conditions and attainments, is exposed condition. The devil may *visit* the highlands and mountain ranges of spiritual elevation, but he makes his *home* in the lowlands. He will attack the strongest, maturest giant form of piety, but he works his havoc and gains his spoils where the Christian slumbers in the cradle of spiritual babyhood. There is no safety but in high aims, strenuous effort and constant advance.

It is on the field of low aims and satisfied results, that the devil wins his chief victories. A spiritual growth, constant and sure spiritual development, is the surest safeguard against Satan's wiles, assaults and surprises. Constant growth is all eyes and all strength. Satan never finds it asleep, drowsy nor weak. Onward, upward, is the great battle cry. Constant advance is the steel armour in the fight with the devil.

Israel lost Canaan by not possessing Canaan. Satan has all the vantage ground when we do not maintain the aggressive.

When the Bible sounded the clarion call, " Let us go on unto perfection," it was seeking to arouse a Church which had lost immensely in the vigour, manliness and fighting ability of Christian character by feeding on milk, and indulging in the lazy luxury of being children. It raises a standard and marks a point for them to gain. The point is far ahead, but it is a real point, as real as the point at which their steps had been stayed by a ruinous stay. They are called out of the cradle and away from the nursery to the strength, conflicts and perfection of a royal manhood.

The eulogy on Wesley by a great writer of being " the first of theological statesmen," pays him no high compliment; but his spiritual perception, the man of open, divine vision, is his highest eulogy, and this is evidenced by the fact that he re-echoed the trumpet call of the Bible, and sounded it on every key and in every refrain, and sought to stir into a forward movement the Church, and quicken its members to seek an advanced position, which had not only dropped out of their experience, but out of their hopes and creeds. God gives religion in its beginnings, and these beginnings are glorious; but to be content with the beginnings of religion, is to forfeit not only its possibilities, but is to leave us opened, naked to Satan, a prey to his schemes. Additions to our spiritual capital are the conditions of solvency, and of the retaining of the capital, and is a victory over the devil as well. To stand still in religion is to lose it. To enter into camp at regeneration, is to forfeit regenerating grace. To stop at any other transitional advance station, is to go backward. The weakness of men is inconstancy to a great aim. The drafts of a long and exhaustive strain are intolerable. We are willing to pay the cost of nerves for a great temporal success, but the price is too dear for religious success. The tendency in religion is to be satisfied with rudiments and to die in infancy. Teething time is a perilous time for spiritual babes. The great sin of the Israelites was hugging the shores and not going up to possess the land. The marvellous glory of their entrance into Canaan paled in the lethargy and timidity of their after advance.

A stopping, standing still, a non-growing, non-fighting condition, is a position fully exposed to Satan. Many run well, fight well, but at some point their running and fighting cease. At once spiritual development is arrested and the devil moves at once to an easy victory. This spiritual arrest may be at the initial steps or stages of spiritual life. The raptures and triumph of the first stages may arrest advance and cause a standstill while the cradle is not out of sight, and the steps are unsteady by baby toddling. It is true that Paul calls the Corinthian saints baby saints, but this was the point where their saintship turned back to carnality and lost its odour, sanctity and strength. Their great sin and backslidings were found in their babyhood, not that they began as babes, but that they stayed babes. Baby sainthood is the popular sainthood of these days. To begin as babes is well, but to remain babes forty years is a fearful deformity.

It would be well for us if spiritual arrest belonged only to the high regions of spiritual advance. While not a few, doubtless, of those who have received a great spiritual baptism after the grace of conversion, have crystallized around this point of advance, the far greater number of people and preachers have crystallized around the initials of grace. We may have some specimens of Christian mummies who in size approach to maturity, but the number of the dwarfed and cradled ones is legion.

Spiritual arrest is not confined though to the initial steps. Its life-blood may chill and its step halt at the point of highest advance. Many Christians are so enthusiastic over some marked advance, some higher elevation gained, that they become enchanted with the beautiful and lofty regions, and are lulled to sleep, and, like Bunyan's Pilgrim, lose their roll, and are all unconscious of their loss; and instead of pressing on with tireless steps, they but cover the future with their imaginations, and while their fancies are filled with the rich colourings of their advanced position, their feet have declined and are in the vale again. They are so happy that it is almost impossible to bring them to their senses, and make them understand that there is many a weary and toilsome step between their Red Sea deliverance and the Promised Land, and that even after the desert is crossed, and the Jordan divided, and the sanctified soil of Canaan pressed by sanctified feet, there is many a battle to be fought, and many an enemy to be destroyed before the goodly land is all possessed. A singing and shouting sanctification is good, but if it is not joined with a marching and fighting sanctification, it will sing and shout itself as thin as a ghost and as dry as a chuck. "Forgetting those things which are behind and reaching forth to those things that are before," is the divine process to hold what we have by getting more. Paul's marvellous career was simple, not complex. He sums it up in fighting, running, watching, the three elements of continuous advance. Many a great battle has been lost by the demoralizing effects of the halt caused by a partial victory in the earlier part of the conflict. It is no easy matter to keep place and march in rank when the spoils of a half-gained victory cover the ground. There is no position this side of heaven free from the dangers of spiritual arrest and secure from the devil's attacks. The conflict and vigilance of advance must mark every step till our feet are within the pearly gates.

A non-growing piety, with an arrested spiritual development, whether the arrest is in the initial stages or at the more advanced steps, is always and everywhere an exposed position, always vulnerable to Satan's attacks.

XV

OUR DEFENSE AGAINST THE DEVIL

Bid me of men beware,
  And to my ways take heed,
Discern their every secret snare,
  And circumspectly tread:
O may I calmly wait
  Thy succours from above,
And stand against their open hate,
  And well-dissembled love!

He that with Christian armour manfully fights against and repels the temptations and assaults of his spiritual enemies, and he that keeps his conscience void of offense, shall enjoy peace here and forever.—*Ray.*

FILL up and crowd out. Leave no room for the devil. Be too busy for him. Have no time and no place for him. Vacant places invite him. The devil loves a vacuum. A very busy person himself, he does his biggest business with those who have no business. The apostle in writing to the Ephesians gives this direction: " Neither give place to the devil." Leave no opening, no space for him. Keep him out by prepossession. Keep him out, nose, head, and all. " Give him an inch he will take an ell."

" Give no place to the devil." The apostle is writing of wrath, which is wicked, by which we give full scope to the devil. He comes into power and has full sway when we relinquish ourselves to the indulgence and continuance of evil passion. Our bad passions are the regions where Satan finds his favourite field and largest sphere of operation. Suppress evil, every tendency to indignation, bitterness and wrath. Suppress and purge out every heated impulse, every unholy flame, every stirring that is not of God. The devil's occupation will then be gone, when gentleness and benignity reign in the spirit.

"Resist the devil and he will flee from you." This is James' curt directory for getting rid of the devil. Resist means to set one's self against, to withstand. Yield him nothing at any point, but oppose him at every point. Be always against him, belonging ever to the party of the opposition as far as his plans, suggestions and ways are concerned. Bravely and strongly to resist what the devil proposes is half victory. To hesitate is to lose. To parley is to yield, to give an inch is the surrender of the whole ground. Firmness, decision and opposition, these the devil cannot stand. He is easily defeated if we are decided and uncompromising. Loyalty to God is rout and ruin to Satan.

We are taught the same simple all important lesson in Peter, with an addition: "Be sober, be vigilant, because your adversary, the devil, as a roaring lion, walketh about, seeking whom he may devour; Whom resist steadfast in the faith, knowing that the same afflictions are accomplished in your brethren that are in the world." The first part of the direction has reference to the elements of personal character. What we are, is of prime consideration in this conflict with the devil. Strong, good character is thrice armed. Character tells in all relations, duties and trials, but nowhere is character more telling in its gracious results than in our encounters with Satan.

Sober, calm and collected, free from passion or intemperance, that cannot be clouded or bewildered; always against spiritual dangers and beguilements; vigilant, cautious and active; never to be surprised nor overcome through unwatchfulness or indolence; aroused and wakeful, because of the full apprehension of the presence of an all powerful, all malignant, all cruel foe. This is our strong defense. Here we have James directing us to " resist," to set one's self against the devil, with will and thought, with conscience and heart, with might and main; rigid and firm, in the faith of God; the Word of God held strictly, strongly and rigidly; the truth of God inflexibly held to make one invincible to the devil, yielding to no assault of his, succumbing to no toil, fainting under no affliction, knowing that these trials have been the portion of God's saints in all ages, and by this warfare with the devil we are perfected, stablished, strengthened and settled. " Be sober," says the apostle, for your adversary, the devil, walketh about. This calm, self-collected condition, free from passion, and with the full mastery of all our powers, is one of the elements of successful resistance to Satan. A passionate man is a weak man. A cool head and a calm heart are the conditions of successful contest with the devil. The apostle adds to this sobriety and vigilance. "Be vigilant," he says, watch, give strict attention, be cautious, be active. Vigilance awakens, sobriety arouses and gives fullest strength.

The Apostle James, in his frank, practical, earnest way, says: "Resist the devil, and he will flee from you." Resist means to set yourself against, to have no parley with, make no concession to, meet the devil only to fight him, talk with him only to withstand him. "Whom resist," says Peter, "steadfast in the faith." That is, be solid, firm, rigid in the faith. Be stalwart in orthodoxy, for heterodoxy has no devil, or only a very amiable and young one, and makes no fight against him.

The spirit of forgiveness always maintained and constantly exercised is a supreme defense against the attacks of Satan. An unforgiving spirit is not only Satan's widest door into our hearts, but it is the strongest imitation and warmest welcome. St. Paul not only urges a spirit of forgiveness as a bar to the devil's ingress, but hastens to close the door by his own readiness to forgive even in advance. "To whom ye forgive anything, I forgive also; for if I forgave anything, to whom I forgave it, for your sakes forgave I it in the person of Christ. Lest Satan should get an advantage of us; for we are not ignorant of his devices." A lofty spirit, ready and compliant with the spirit of forgiveness, free from all bitterness, revenge or retaliation, has freed itself from the conditions which invite Satan, and has effectually locked and barred his entrance. The readiest way to keep Satan out is to keep the spirit of forgiveness in. The devil is never deeper in hell nor farther removed from us than when we can pray, " Father, forgive them; they know not what they do."

The devil is to be overcome. He is not only a hypocrite, full of quiet, slippery and artful ways, but he is a man of war, a warrior of renown of many a campaign and many a battle-field. It is not all poetry nor myth that his valour and prowess were tested in heaven. Angels were his foemen there, heaven the scene of his conflict and his defeat, and still he fights. It takes strong young blood with its fire and valour to meet him and conquer.

The devil must be defeated. Victory over him is victory all along the line. It takes strength and valour to overcome him. He is no baby foe, no disheartened enemy. The ardour and valour of a manly faith is requisite in this battle. The Word of God is the conquering sword in this warfare. He who has his quiver full of these divine arrows, swift, strong, penetrating and deadly to Satan and to sin, will be more than conqueror over the devil.

The weapon used by the Son of God in His conflict with Satan was the Word of God, and by it He conquered.

"I have written unto you, young men, because ye are strong, and the word of God abideth in you, and ye have overcome the wicked one." The John of love, nearest the heart and deepest in the Spirit of his Lord, is full of this victory. John's love was too genuine to evaporate itself into sickly sentiment, or evaporate the devil into a mere influence. His experience was too profound, his memory too quick and retentive for an impersonal devil or an impersonal Christ. He had the scars of the battles with the adversary of his soul. He had witnessed the conflicts of many a young soldier. His soul had shared in their triumph and recorded their victories. Fight the devil and overcome him, is John's process of becoming fathers in spiritual power, rooted, grounded and perfected. Overcoming the devil, is with John the presage of overcoming the world.

The mighty new-birth principle makes a man watchful like a sentinel at his post, when the enemy in power is massed in the front, like a watchman on the walls of a beleaguered city and like a guard over a royal prisoner. This keeping and guarding himself, is safety against Satan's inflaming touch. As with his Lord, so the faithful, vigilant Christian keeps himself, and Satan comes and finds nothing in him. Every point is barred and sleeplessly watched. " We know that whatsoever is born of God sinneth not; but he that is begotten of God keepeth himself, and that wicked one toucheth him not. And we know that we are of God, and the whole world lieth in the evil one." " Keeping ourselves " is the surest pledge that Satan will not keep us. Hands on ourselves in holy vigilance keeps Satan's hands off. The martyr spirits who are faithful unto death, who love not their lives unto death, are victors in this warfare with the devil: "And I heard a loud voice saying in heaven, Now is come salvation, and strength, and the kingdom of our God, and the power of his Christ; for the accuser of our brethren is cast down, which accused them before our God day and night. And they overcame him by the blood of the Lamb, and by the word of their testimony; and they loved not their lives unto the death." The blood of the everlasting covenant must be sprinkled on the warriors who are victors against Satan. A clear conscious experience of the saving power of that blood and an ability to be a martyr-witness before any company at any cost mark their devotion to Christ and their experience of His salvation. " He is mine and I am his."

Satan cannot stand an exposition of the blood of Christ. He turns pale at every view of Calvary. The flowing wounds are the signals of his retreat. A heart sprinkled with the blood is holy ground, on which he not only dares not tread, but he dreads and trembles and cowers in the presence of the blood-besprinkled warrior.

A clear-ringing word of testimony as to the power of that blood, he fears more than the attack of a legion of archangels. It is like the charge of an irresistible phalanx which bears everything down before it. It is the blood applied and the testimony to its application, the martyr witness in life and by tongue of the power of that blood is more a barrier against Satan than a wall of fire. The atoning blood, an experience of that blood— that is heaven's infallible protection against Satan. They in heaven thus overcame the devil. We also " overcome him by the blood of the Lamb and the word of our testimony."

No sorrow is so pathetic as the sorrow of young widowhood, which is an exposed sorrow, as we have seen, to Satan's attacks. Paul's direction puts them on the defensive and guards them against the insidious attacks of the enemy. I quote from the Revised Version: " I will therefore that the young widows marry, bear children, guide the house, give none occasion to the adversary to speak reproachfully. For some are already turned aside after Satan." No defense is more secure against Satan than a life crowned and crowded with sweetest duties all so fully discharged as to give no occasion to the devil to speak reproachfully.

The devil's work is much helped or much hindered by the spirit of the servants of Christ. Gentleness becomes the servants of Christ not only as a beautiful adorning, but as the corner foundation stone. Meekness and gentleness win men, for they form the Christly character. Sharpness, impatience and contention are no spiritual propaganda, neither are they good recruiting officers for Christ. " And the servant of the Lord must not strive, but be gentle unto all men, apt to teach, patient; in meekness instructing those that oppose themselves; if God peradventure will give them repentance to the acknowledging of the truth. And that they may recover themselves out of the snare of the devil, who are taken captive by him at his will." A very passionate preacher is long-suffering doctrine.

" Watch " is the keynote of safety. The devil plies us by a thousand instruments, comes to us in a thousand ways, administers a thousand rebukes, and assaults by a thousand surprises. Wakefulness at all times is our only safety, wide-awake not only when we see his form and fear his presence, but wide-awake to see him when he is not to be seen, to repel him when he comes in any one of his ten thousand guises or disguises—this is our wise and safe course.

No alarm cry is so frequent in the New Testament as the call to watch. No call hurts Satan so vitally and none defeats him so readily and so totally as to watch. Being on the watch tower prevents all surprises, and is the presage of victory at all times.

The Son of God makes it the keynote to many a solemn saying. It is a call to be sleepless, to vigilance, to be ready, always ready. It is an image drawn from shepherds, in which we have Jacob's indignant defense and protest against Laban: " In the day the drought consumed me and the frost by night and sleep departed from mine eyes." To watch is to be opposed to all listlessness, a wakeful state, sleep gone. It implies a wakeful state, as the rousing effort in the presence of some great peril, cautious, wary, a state untouched by any slumbering or beclouding influence. Drowsiness and bewilderment are gone. It quickens us against laziness and spiritual sloth.

Read how the church at Sardis is called to the exercise of watchfulness, because she was stupefied by the opiates of a fair exterior and a goodly religious frame. The Ephesian Church is charged to unite watching with persevering prayer. The Corinthian Church is urged to watch and stand fast. The Colossians are exhorted to " continue in prayer and watch in the same." The Thessalonians are to " watch and be sober." Timothy, the young preacher, was to " watch in all things." Peter's call is " to be sober, and watch unto prayer," because the solemn end of all things was hastening. Again he says: " Be sober; be vigilant; because your adversary, the devil, as a roaring lion, walketh about seeking whom he might devour." In Revelation we have the startling call, "Behold I come as a thief. Blessed is he that watcheth and keepeth his garments, lest he walk naked, and they see his shame."

The most frequent call to watchfulness is from our Lord. "Watch, therefore," He says, "for ye know not what hour your Lord doth come." Again He calls us to the exercise of this great grace, "Watch, therefore, for ye know neither the day nor the hour the Son of Man cometh." Again and again does He call us "to watch ye therefore." The herald cry, the trumpet call from Him to us, is to be awake, to be fully awake, to be tremendously awake. "Watch ye, therefore, and pray always, that ye may be accounted worthy to escape all these things that shall come to pass and to stand before the Son of Man." "Watch and pray," He charged His disciples, and so He charges us to "Watch and pray, that ye enter not into temptation; the spirit indeed is willing, but the flesh is weak." Still the flesh is weak, and watchfulness must ever be united with prayer while we are in the flesh.

XVI

OUR DEFENSE AGAINST THE DEVIL
(Continued)

> Soldiers of Christ arise,
>   And put your armour on,
> Strong in the strength which God supplies
>   Through His eternal Son;
> Strong in the Lord of Hosts,
>   And in His mighty power,
> Who in the strength of Jesus trusts,
>   Is more than conqueror.
>
> Stand then in His great might,
>   With all His strength endued;
> But take, to arm you for the fight,
>   The panoply of God;
> That having all things done,
>   And all your conflicts past,
> Ye may o'ercome through Christ alone,
>   And stand entire at last.

HOW many prayers have missed the mark and been in vain because not mixed with wary vigilance. How many sad failures in Christian life because watchfulness failed. The devil has no readier prey than a sleepy Christian. Bunyan's Christian lost his roll when he fell asleep. Many Christians, not in allegory, but in fact, have lost their souls by the same failure. Eternal vigilance is the price of political liberty. No less a price must be paid for our spiritual safety. The foolish virgins missed heaven because they failed in this grace. Watchfulness would have brought them with the Bridegroom into the high joys of heaven's festal hour.

In the sixth chapter of Ephesians, we have the whole warfare with the devil and his legions, and the sources of defense and victory:

"Finally, my brethren, be strong in the Lord, and in the power of his might. Put on the whole armour of God, that ye may be able to stand against the wiles of the devil. For we wrestle not against flesh and blood, but against principalities, against powers, against the rulers of the darkness of this world, against spiritual wickedness in high places. Wherefore, take unto you the whole armour of God, that ye may be able to withstand in the evil day, and having done all, to stand. Stand, therefore, having your loins girt about with truth, and having on the breastplate of righteousness; and your feet shod with the preparation of the gospel of peace. Above all, taking the shield of faith, wherewith ye shall be able to quench all the fiery darts of the wicked. And take the helmet of salvation, and the sword of the Spirit, which is the Word of God. Praying always with all prayer and supplication in the Spirit and watching thereunto with all perseverance and supplication for all saints. And for me that utterance may be given unto me, that I may open my mouth boldly, to make known the mystery of the gospel. For which I am an ambassador in bonds; that therein I may speak boldly, as I ought to speak." In this passage we have a view of the strenuous conflict and of the battle-field on which the issues of eternity are tossed.

The Christian's battle is with the devil and his wiles or methods. His struggle is arranged with order, wisdom and skill. Principalities and powers are under his management and subject to his orders, they, the first and the highest, the first in creation and the highest in dignity. They are his lieutenants, his prime ministers, his captain generals, to carry out his orders and represent him fully. They are the world rulers, world-wide, world-powerful. They master and control all the evil forces of the world. The devil and his higher confederates are world-rulers. Their might is co-extensive with the world. A mighty sway is theirs, a fearful rule for evil, against the good and against man. Their subordinates, the rank and file, are innumerable and invincible, save to a God-equipped man. What a vast and powerful array of enemies are there, aggressive, malignant and cruel. They are high or in heavenly places, the very place where Christ's power is located. This power is over us, above us and around us. They are too mighty for us. Against this invisible, innumerable, all-powerful and vast array, we *wrestle*. A close conflict is wrestling. An intense and arduous conflict it is, strenuous, which tests all strength and strains every fiber. It is hand to hand, foot to foot, close contact, a grappling. It is not with men, though men may give us much opposition in our Christian course. But our chief trouble, our main trouble, our great war, is not with man but with all the mighty evil forces of the devil. A life and death struggle it is, a war for heaven and hell, for time and eternity.

The Christian must be a soldier by birth, by fortune, by trade. The best elements of a divine soldiership must be his, "not entangled with the affairs of this life." Princely in the elements and measure of self-denial, courage and endurance, are the engraved characteristics of this soldierhood. Strength is the fruit of these high qualities. But strength far beyond his own strength. "Strong in the Lord, and in the power of his might." For the preparation for this war the Christian soldier must go out of himself. The strength of God, the very strength of God's almightiness, must be his. The ability to stand, to fight, to conquer and to drive the foe from the field, will be found in God's armour. God's strength is imparted through God's armour. No power short of God can enable us to meet the devil. No partial equipment will suffice. We are charged twice to make it doubly sure to take the *whole* armour. We take God by taking His armour. We have God by having put the armour on us. Make His armour our own. We put on God by putting on His armour. Not outside but inside, not objective but subjective, not imputed only, but inwrought. Christ made the armour, the Holy Spirit fits and puts it on us, and makes it ours. We have to fight through to the end and drive the foe and hold the battle-field, and having done all, to stand. First withstand, and then stand. We gain and hold, and then advance. Stand ready for the fight, stand in the fight.

Strong and valorous for the truth, in the inward parts; no sham soldier, no sham fighting. All is real and true. Being truthful, a girded soldier, strong and tucked up and narrowed to the intensest and deepest form of truth, his girdle the truth, for truth is the band, the ornament of a jewelled girdle, a diamond set in gold. We must conquer the devil by truth as the strength and support of our lives. We know the truth and have the truth, for we have Christ who is the truth.

"The breastplate of righteousness." Heart righteousness makes head righteousness and life righteousness. We cannot fight without heart righteousness. The "breastplate of righteousness" protects the heart and makes us feel right. The old heart cannot be made right by the most skillful artificer nor by the most correct doing. No tinkering on the old heart can make it right. It is as hard as a stone and crooked as the Jordan, and no melting can make it soft and no human effort can make it straight. A new heart soft as flesh and washed whiter than snow in the blood of Christ, a copy and a piece of Christ's heart, " perfect, and right, and pure, and good "—this is what is needed.

The feet must be shod with a preparation which is always ready to go, to do and to suffer. Slow movements, a dilatory doing of God's will, being off guard, a general unreadiness for life or death, for earth or heaven, for sacrifice or service, for doing or for suffering, cuts the nerves of Christian valour and lays us open to surprises and crushing defeats. Always ready is the soldier attitude of safety, and ready to move presages victory. Flying columns are Satan's most dreaded foes. Wakeful vigilance is assured victory against the devil.

The " shield of faith " is the all-important and the all-covering article of armour. The devil lets fly his fiery, poisoned darts, but faith catches them as they are directed to head or heart, and arrests and quenches them. Dost thou believe all victories are possible to the soldier, valiant and strong in faith? No battle was ever planned by hell's most gifted strategist which can conquer faith. All its inflamed and terrible darts fall harmless as they strike against the shield of faith. " These all died in faith." Faith made their death the crowning point. Faith brought to their dying hour the spoils of their victories.

" The helmet " protects the head. Bear in mind that head-salvation and heart-salvation, real and

full, are stronger than brass to protect the head.
A heart fully saved holds the head to truth and
righteousness, like the anchor holds the ship in
stormiest seas. "The *hope* of salvation," says
Paul in Thessalonians, is the helmet. The Christian soldier must put heaven strongly in his head
and heart. He must see heaven, feel heaven and
keep heaven in the eye and in the heart all the time.
He will stand with unsteady step if heaven be far
off. He will fight feebly if heaven be seen dimly.
The full sight of heaven will give strength to his
loins, ardour to his faith, glory to his future and
victory to the present. The head will never be
pierced while hope is its helmet. Nurture hope,
strengthen hope and brighten hope, for we are
"saved by hope." We must "abound in hope"
by the power of the Holy Spirit.

"The sword," the aggressive and powerful
weapon, is the Word of God. The Spirit wields it
in death to all our foes. The Word of God is our
battle-field and victorious weapon. On it we stand
and fight. With it we deal rout and ruin to every
foe. The Christian soldier is " not to live by bread
alone but by every word of God." We cannot
make too much of the Word of God. Christ foiled
Satan with it. If we be valiant, true and invincible, we also must have the Word of God dwelling in us richly. The shield of our faith, and the
shape and form of that shield, is the basis of our
prayers, the granite and essence of our girded

truth. Head and hands and heart must be filled, impregnated and surcharged with God's Word; by it we live and by it we grow. It is our battle call, and the sign by which we conquer. A glittering royal blade it is in all the assaults of Satan. *"It is written,"* goes like steel to the heart of Satan. As a weapon of defense and offense, God has magnified His Word above all His name. Thrice armed against all Satan's wiles and his devices, are those who are filled with God's Word. It is " quick and powerful and sharper than any two-edged sword, piercing even to the dividing asunder of soul and spirit," and Satan feels it penetrating his joints and marrow, dissolving into weakness all his strength and making poor and foolish all his wisest plans.

The soldiers in the warfare against the devil must understand how to wear the armour of all prayer. " All prayer " in all kinds, and at all seasons, in the intensest form, with deepest sense of personal need of God, is the demand. Prayer must deepen and narrow and intensify into supplications, helped into this mighty praying, clothed with this resistless power of prayer by the Holy Spirit. This intense conflict with the devil requires sleepless vigilance, midnight vigils, a wakefulness which cannot be surprised, a perseverance which knows neither halting, fainting, nor depression, which knows by clearest spiritual intelligence what it needs, and what the illimitable provisions are to supply all those needs, and the imperative necessity of pressing the prayer till the need is supplied and the succour is secured. This praying holds itself in loving sympathy with the entire family of God, making their conflicts, perils and needs its own. It is in line of battle with the whole familyhood of God, taking in their foes, their safety and their perils. " Supplication for all saints " gives victory to every saint. The line of battle is one. Defeat or victory must come to all. It is the soldier fully equipped in God's armour, who is a veteran against the devil and invincible to all of his attacks.

It is not an easy thing to pray. Back of the praying there must lie the conditions of prayer. These conditions are possible, but they are not to be seized on in a moment by the prayerless. Present they always may be to the faithful and holy, but cannot exist in nor be met by a frivolous, negligent and laggard spirit. Prayer does not stand alone. It is not an isolated performance. Prayer stands in closest connection with all the duties of an ardent piety. It is the issuance of a character which is made up of the elements of a vigorous and commanding faith. Prayer honours God, acknowledges His being, exalts His power, adores His providence and secures His aid. A sneering half-rationalism cries out against devotion, and charges that it does nothing but pray. But to pray well, is to do all things well. If it be true that devotion does nothing but pray, then it does nothing at all. To do nothing but pray fails to do the praying, for the antecedent, coincident and subsequent conditions of prayer are but the sum of all the energized forces of a practical working piety.

Prayer puts God in the matter with commanding force. " Ask of me things to come concerning my sons," says God, " and concerning the work of my hands, command ye me." We are charged in God's Word, " always to pray," " in everything by prayer," " continuing instant in prayer," to " pray everywhere," " praying always." The promise is as illimitable as the command is comprehensive. " All things whatsoever ye shall ask in prayer believing ye shall receive." " Whatsoever ye shall ask;" ' if ye shall ask anything;" " Ye shall ask what ye will and it shall be done unto you." " Whatsoever ye ask the Father he will give it you." If there is anything not involved in " All things whatsoever," or not found in the phrase, " Ask anything," then these things may be left out of prayer. Language could not cover a wider range, nor involve more fully all minutia. These statements are but samples of the all-comprehending possibilities of prayer under the promises of God to those who meet the conditions of right praying.

These passages, though, give but a general outline of the immense regions over which prayer extends its sway. Beyond these the effect of prayer reaches and secures good from regions which cannot be traversed by language or thought. Paul exhausted language and thought in praying, but conscious of necessities not covered, and realms of good not reached, of battles not gained over enemies and not conquered, he covers these impenetrable and undiscovered regions by this general plea: "Unto him that is able to do exceeding abundantly above all that we ask or think, according to the power that worketh in us." The promise is, "Call unto me, and I will answer thee, and show thee great and mighty things, which thou knowest not."